THE SCHWEICH LECTURES ON
BIBLICAL ARCHAEOLOGY, 1932

RECENT DEVELOPMENTS
IN THE
TEXTUAL CRITICISM
OF THE GREEK BIBLE

RECENT DEVELOPMENTS
IN THE
TEXTUAL CRITICISM
OF THE GREEK BIBLE

BY

FREDERIC G. KENYON, F.B.A.

Late Director and Principal Librarian
of the British Museum

THE SCHWEICH LECTURES
OF THE BRITISH ACADEMY
1932

LONDON
PUBLISHED FOR THE BRITISH ACADEMY
BY HUMPHREY MILFORD, OXFORD UNIVERSITY PRESS
AMEN HOUSE, E.C.
1933

OXFORD UNIVERSITY PRESS
AMEN HOUSE, E.C. 4
LONDON EDINBURGH GLASGOW
LEIPZIG NEW YORK TORONTO
MELBOURNE CAPETOWN BOMBAY
CALCUTTA MADRAS SHANGHAI
HUMPHREY MILFORD
PUBLISHER TO THE
UNIVERSITY

PRINTED IN GREAT BRITAIN

PREFACE

THE special occasion of the course of Schweich Lectures published in this volume was the recent discovery of the Chester Beatty Biblical papyri, which added very largely to the material available for the textual criticism of the Greek Bible, and seemed likely to throw valuable light on the early history of the text. Since the publication of these papyri must inevitably take some considerable time, the summary and provisional account of them in the present volume may be of interest to scholars; but in the main the lectures were addressed less to specialists than to ordinary students of the Bible. It seemed a convenient opportunity to summarize for such students the main results of discovery and criticism since the publication of Westcott and Hort's *Introduction* to their edition of the New Testament (1882), and Swete's *Introduction to the Old Testament in Greek* (1900). Much of the work, therefore, is secondhand, embodying the results of the work of others, to whom, it is hoped, full acknowledgement has in all cases been made. In a sense, the present volume is a supplement to my previous works, addressed to the same class of readers: *The Bible and the Ancient Manuscripts* (1895, 3rd ed., revised, 1898) and *Handbook to the Textual Criticism of the New Testament* (1901, 2nd ed., revised, 1912). It is hoped it may be found useful until the new material has been more thoroughly worked over and digested by specialists, and that it may perhaps encourage some younger scholars to devote themselves to this field of study, in which new recruits are much needed.

It had been expected that the publication of the first and most important of the new papyri (the Gospels and Acts MS.) would have preceded that of the present volume; but various causes have delayed it, and seem likely to reverse the order of appearance. The other papyri are approximately ready for the press, and should follow as fast as printing can be undertaken.

F. G. K.

28 *March*, 1933.

CONTENTS

CHAPTER I

WESTCOTT AND HORT AND THE REVISED VERSION

THE publication of the edition of the Greek New Testament by Westcott and Hort, just over fifty years ago, in May 1881, was in the strictest sense of the term an epoch in the history of the textual criticism of the Bible. It was a point of pause, of summing up results achieved, a starting-point for fresh study and further advance. Things after it could never be the same as they were before. All subsequent critics and students, alike in this country and abroad, whether they accepted or rejected its conclusions, were bound to take notice of them, and to give their reasons for accepting or rejecting the principles on which they were founded. For the ordinary English reader of the Bible the same epoch is marked by the practically simultaneous publication of the Revised Version of the New Testament. On 17 May of that year Paternoster Row and the adjoining streets were congested with the wagons and lorries gathered to carry away and distribute this new version of the Bible in English, which was to introduce the ordinary reader for the first time to at any rate a large portion of the results to which the critical methods of Westcott and Hort led. It was a severe shock, the character and causes of which were largely misunderstood at the time, and perhaps are not universally understood now. Whether right or wrong in principle, whether accepted or not accepted, the Revised Version was an outstanding landmark in the history of the English Bible.

The year 1881, consequently, marks the end of one period in the history of New Testament textual criticism and the beginning of another. Of such periods, if one surveys the course of that history to the present day, one may reckon six, of very unequal lengths, including that in which we find ourselves to-day.

B

The first is that which extends from the dates of composition of the several books of the New Testament, in the latter half of the first century, to the acceptance of Christianity by Constantine, for which the most convenient date is A.D. 325. During this period the several books circulated in manuscripts written on papyrus, under the shadow of periodical persecution and destruction of copies, with restricted command of scholarship and of material resources, and with little opportunity for the comparison of copies produced in different parts of the world or for the maintenance of a uniform text. It is in this period that all the textual problems were created which criticism has endeavoured, and still endeavours, to solve. Of this period there will be much to say later in this course of lectures; for it is to it that the discoveries of recent years, which are my principal subject and the cause of the existence of these lectures, relate.

The second period extends from the acceptance of Christianity to the first appearance of the Greek New Testament in print; in other words, from 325 to 1516. It covers the whole of what we commonly call the Middle Ages. It is also the period of the vogue of the vellum manuscript codex. Every copy of the Greek Bible produced during this period was written by hand, and all except a very few were written on vellum; a few in the earlier portion of it on papyrus, and more towards the end of it on paper. Thousands of copies of the Greek Bible written during this period have survived to our own day, a still larger number of the Latin translation known as the Vulgate, and smaller quantities of translations into other languages, Syriac, Egyptian, Ethiopic, Armenian, Georgian, Persian, and others. It was a period of the transmission of texts, not, except to a very small extent, of the critical revision of them. It gave us the immense number of copies (totally unrivalled by any other book in all the literature of the ancient world) with which textual scholars have to deal to-day; but it did nothing for their critical evaluation and classification. The Bible was the Bible, and few scholars troubled themselves to question the accuracy of the copies produced, or to inquire after the original form of the sacred texts.

The third period is that of the establishment of the accepted form of the printed text of the Greek New Testament. It begins with the first New Testament of Erasmus in 1516 and the Complutensian Polyglot by Ximenes of the complete Greek Bible in 1522, and ends with the first Elzevir edition of 1624. Its result was the establishment of the Received Text, the Textus Receptus, which for two centuries and a half was the universally accepted form of the Greek Scriptures.[1] For English readers it is also the period of the formation of the English Bible, starting with Tyndale's New Testament in 1525, and culminating in the Authorized Version of 1611, which represents the Textus Receptus in an English dress.

The fourth period extends from this date to 1831. It is the period of the collection of materials for the criticism of the text embodied in the Textus Receptus. In 1627 the Codex Alexandrinus was brought from Constantinople to England, and the critical examination and comparison of manuscripts began. Scholars such as Walton (1657), Fell (1675), Mill (1707), Bentley (who never arrived at publication of his results), Bengel (1734), Wetstein (1751–2), Griesbach (1774–1806), Matthaei (1782–8), and Scholz (1830–6) collected, collated, and described hundreds of Greek MSS., and formed regular *apparatus critici* for the examination of the text. Their great service was the accumulation of material rather than the critical use of it. Only by Bengel, Semler (1764–7), and Griesbach was any considerable attempt made to draw constructive conclusions from the mass of material collected.

[1] The phrase *textus receptus* occurs first in the preface to the second Elzevir edition of 1633. The standard forms of the Textus Receptus are the third edition of Stephanus (R. Estienne) in 1550, and the Elzevir of 1624.

The fifth period covers the half-century from 1831 to 1881, and represents the first period of constructive criticism. The great names in it are those of Lachmann, Tischendorf, and Tregelles. It was mainly through their labours that opinion was led to the point of realizing the necessity of a revision of the Textus Receptus; and these labours were brought to a head by Westcott and Hort. It is the conclusions at which they arrived that form the basis from which the present inquiry takes its start.

The object of this series of lectures is to review the progress that has been made in textual criticism since 1881, during the fifty years which, so far, constitute our sixth period. It is an attempt to make more intelligible and more widely known among the general public interested in Biblical studies the work done by a large number of specialists. During this half-century many interesting and important discoveries of new manuscripts have been made, and much intensive study has been devoted to the material previously available. It is the results of these discoveries and studies that I shall try to summarize. It is obvious that to the specialist the greater part of what I have to say will be already familiar. It is only towards the end, in dealing with the latest discoveries of all, that I may have something new to contribute. But the Schweich Lectures are intended not only to embody original research, but also to make generally known the results of research. Even to researchers it may be of service from time to time to gather up and survey the results achieved by a number of different workers over a substantial period of time, and to try to discover the main trend of opinion, the ground definitely made good, and the directions in which further progress is possible or probable. But for the most part I claim no more than to be using the work of others, in the hope of making it known to those who have not hitherto been brought into contact with it.

I shall be dealing mainly with the text of the New Testament, on which more work has been done and of which there is more to record; but in the final chapter I propose also to give some account of the progress of Septuagint studies.

These last fifty years constitute, then, the beginning of the sixth of the periods into which I have divided the history of the New Testament text. The end of the period remains to be fixed by those who will come after, perhaps by some future Schweich Lecturer. In order to understand them, it is necessary first to set out at some length the point at which the study had arrived at the beginning of the period, at the time when Westcott and Hort's text and the Revised Version of the New Testament set the seal on the work of the previous generation.

So far back as the days of Bengel, in the second quarter of the eighteenth century, the principle had been enunciated that the total mass of textual authorities (including both manuscripts in the original tongue and translations into other languages) must be divided into certain distinct groups, at least into a small group of the most ancient authorities, and a much larger group containing nearly all those of later date. This principle was extended by Semler and his pupil Griesbach, the latter of whom classified the authorities for the Gospels into three groups, which he named Alexandrian, Western, and Constantino-politan, the last, which he regarded as a relatively late outgrowth from the other two, including the great majority of extant manuscripts.

The theory of Westcott and Hort (I apologize for this recapitulation of familiar matter) was essentially on the same lines as that of Griesbach. By their time the mass of available evidence had been greatly increased, and in particular two manuscripts of primary importance had been brought to light. The Codex Vaticanus had been made known after nearly four hundred years of obscurity in the Vatican Library, and the Codex Sinaiticus had been discovered by Tischendorf and brought from Sinai to St. Petersburg. Westcott and Hort divided all their textual witnesses into four classes, to which they gave distinctive names; (1) *Neutral*, headed and indeed overwhelmingly dominated by the Vaticanus, with much support from the Sinaiticus and a small number of other authorities, and supposed to be of Egyptian origin; (2) *Alexandrian*, comprising a small number of witnesses who could also be domiciled in Egypt but who did not conform to the Neutral type; (3) *Western*, of which the leading representatives were the Codex Bezae, the Old Latin version, and the Curetonian Syriac, and whose origin was to be looked for in Rome; and (4) *Syrian*, so called because the type was supposed to have originated in or about Antioch, and thence to have spread over the whole Greek world, and to include the immense majority of extant MSS.

Hort's line of argument may be briefly recapitulated as follows. In the early days of the Church, absolute fidelity of transcription was little valued. Scribes felt themselves at liberty to vary the words of the Gospels, to smooth away roughnesses or obscurities of style, to assimilate the narratives of the Evangelists when recording the same events, and at times to incorporate incidents or words from other sources. Hence there came into existence, as early as the second century, a type of text characterized by very free departures from the true tradition. This type took root in the Syriac Church, but was carried from the East to the West, and being best known from its appearance in Latin authorities may be named *Western*. In spite of its very early origin its testimony is not to be highly regarded, on account of the liberties which it takes with the text; and a reading attested wholly or mainly by Western authorities must, according to Hort, be regarded with the gravest suspicion. At the same time in Egypt, the home of classical culture, the type of text which he designates as *Alexandrian* was coming into existence as the result of minor verbal alterations due to a sense of literary style and a desire to smooth away roughnesses of expression. Subsequently, the growing diversity and confusion of Greek texts led, in his view, to an authoritative revision at Antioch, perhaps in two stages, which about the middle of the fourth century culminated in the type of text which he calls *Syrian*, and which rapidly gained universal popularity and thenceforward dominated the tradition of the New Testament text. This version was marked by harmonistic assimilation of parallel texts, by the combination or conflation of variant readings, by additions of pronouns, conjunctions, and other expletives, and by a general obliteration of characteristic individualisms of style. It was smooth, full, and easy, and consequently won a very general acceptance. From this nearly universal corruption only a few manuscripts escaped, of which by far the most trustworthy, as well as the earliest, is the Codex Vaticanus; and to this and its small group of followers is reserved the title of *Neutral*, signifying that here predominantly we are to find the pure tradition of the New Testament text.

In this conclusion, giving emphatic preference to a few early manuscripts over an overwhelming mass of later date, there is in principle nothing novel. On the contrary, it is a commonplace in the textual criticism of ancient classical authors. Editors have long been accustomed to rely mainly on a very small number of manuscripts, or even not infrequently on one alone, in preference to the numerically preponderant majority of later authorities. When applied, however, to the text of the New Testament, and resulting as it did in a large number of small alterations in very familiar passages, it gave a very disagreeable shock to a public unfamiliar with the processes of textual science. The Revised New Testament consequently encountered a storm of adverse criticism. The leader of the attack was Dean Burgon, who to his undoubted learning united great powers of incisive invective. The early years of our period were accordingly occupied by the controversy between the Received Text and Hort's Neutral Text. Burgon and his followers relied on the immense numerical preponderance of the witnesses for the Received

Text, which they took as embodying the deliberate judgement of the Church, while they regarded the Vatican and Sinaitic codices, with their few allies, as scanty survivals of a corrupt tradition, which perhaps owed their survival to their very badness.

Against this appeal to numbers the supporters of Hort, among whom were included the large majority of trained textual critics, opposed the principles of criticism and a detailed examination of the evidence. The crux of the controversy lay in the testimony of the ancient Fathers. Hort's contention, which was the corner-stone of his theory, was that readings characteristic of the Received Text are never found in the quotations of Christian writers prior to about A.D. 350. Before that date we find characteristically 'Neutral' and 'Western' readings, but never 'Syrian'. This argument is in fact decisive; and no subsequent discovery of new witnesses, and no further examination of the old, has invalidated it. It would be superfluous to recapitulate here the course of the controversy, which was heated but short. When once the weight of this argument is realized, and when it is also understood that the critical method proposed is in accordance with the general principles and practice of the criticism of ancient texts, the controversy is at an end. No scholar trained in textual criticism would now uphold, or has for many years past upheld, the superiority of the Received Text as compared with the earlier witnesses. It would serve no good purpose to exhume the dead or to re-slay the slain. Those who are interested in an extinct controversy can find it in the handbooks of thirty and forty years ago.

It survives only in one form, where it still does much mischief, namely in the general attitude towards the Revised Version. That Version, though continuing in steady use, especially by careful students of the Bible, has never become popular. It has not replaced the Authorized Version, as the Authorized Version replaced the Bishops' and the Geneva Bibles; and it is still the object of much hostile criticism. It should be understood, however, that there are two totally distinct grounds on which it may be, and has been, attacked. One is the argument that the Greek text on which it is based was wrongly chosen, that it was an error to depart from the traditional 'Received Text'. The other is that in English style and in command of language it is inferior to the Authorized Version, and that it is guilty of pedantic neglect of idiom and an imperfect comprehension of the idiosyncrasies of the Greek prevalent at the time and in the places in which the New Testament books were written. Now the second of these grounds of criticism is admissible, but the first is not. It is certainly true that (owing in part to the discoveries of Greek papyri during the last fifty years) more is known about the Greek of the first century than was known to the Revisers. It is also possible to question some of the axioms of translation adopted by the Revisers, and to hold that as masters of the English language they were not the equals of Tyndale and Coverdale and King James's translators. Where, therefore, divergences between the Authorized Version and the Revised depend on points of style, criticism is legitimate. Where, however, they are due to differences in the text translated, it must be recognized that the presumption is overwhelmingly in favour of the Revision. There is plenty of room for discussion on details and on particular readings still. It would be held by many that the Revisers, owing to a spirit of compromise, did not always go far enough in their rejection of the Received Text. But in general it must be taken as an assured result that the text underlying the Revised Version is superior to that underlying the Authorized. The Authorized Version remains the masterpiece of the English language; but for accuracy of text the Revised must have the preference.

That particular controversy, then, between the Received Text and its rivals is over and done with. But this does not mean that the Greek text of the New Testament is finally settled and universally accepted. So long as the Received

Text was effectively in the field, all the supporters of an earlier type of text could combine against it. But it has sometimes happened in history that when a victory has been won, the allied victors fall out over the spoil; and so it has happened here. The Received Text being removed from the field, differences arose between the various types of earlier texts, fighting at first under the banners of 'Neutral' and 'Western', the titles given to them by Hort. The main problem of criticism during the latter part of our period has been the examination and evaluation of these types of text, and this will have to be dealt with at greater length.

It will probably be convenient first to set out in general the nature of the problems to be examined; next to describe the principal accessions of evidence that have been made within the period under review; and finally to try to sum up the conclusions at which criticism, in the light of the new materials, has arrived, or to which it seems to be tending.

The Neutral text, which bore the brunt of the controversy with the Textus Receptus, is pre-eminently and predominantly the text of the Codex Vaticanus (B). In the opinion not merely of Westcott and Hort but of other scholars who have examined it from a different point of view, its readings (apart from casual scribal errors which are obvious and easily eliminated), when they differ from those of other authorities, can generally be given the preference on grounds of intrinsic probability. This is of course a conclusion open to argument, as to which more may have to be said later; for the moment I am only stating the position of Hort. The text of B, in his view and that of others, shows no sign either of deliberate revision or of free treatment by scribes with loose views as to textual accuracy. It has the appearance of conscientious and accurate tradition; and to it, as to the leading manuscript of many classical authors, the preference should generally be given in cases of variant readings. With it, in the next

place, the Codex Sinaiticus (‎א) is frequently, but not by
any means always, in agreement. Evidently both manuscripts had a common ancestor, not immediate but not
very remote, which carries back the evidence for readings
in which they agree a considerable distance towards the
original autographs. The Sinaiticus, however, has been
affected by another stream of tradition, more akin to the
Western group, which leads it at times to diverge from the
Vaticanus.

With these two primary authorities, of which the Sinaiticus contains the entire New Testament and the Vaticanus
the whole as far as Hebrews ix. 14 (the Pastoral Epistles,
which followed Hebrews, being lost as well as the Apocalypse), are grouped in general agreement a number of fragmentary manuscripts, namely those known as L R T Z Ξ
in the Gospels, Δ and Ψ in Mark, and a handful of minuscules, of which the most noteworthy are 33 in the Gospels
and 81 in the Acts.[1] Among the versions, the Bohairic
comes nearest to it, with considerable support from the
Sahidic. In books other than the Gospels, the Codex
Alexandrinus (A) and the Codex Ephraemi (C) likewise
generally belong to this group. For fuller particulars
reference may be made to the standard handbooks of
textual criticism.

Over against this so-called 'Neutral' group there stood
a number of other authorities, which could equally be
shown, on the evidence of the Fathers, to contain a text
of earlier date than the Receptus, but which differed
markedly from B and its allies. These authorities Hort,
following Griesbach, grouped together under the title of
'Western'. At the time of the publication of the Westcott
and Hort text, the leading champions of this type were
the bilingual Codex Bezae (D), the Old Latin Version
(especially in the earliest form of it represented by the

---

[1] I use throughout the nomenclature of Tischendorf revised and
extended by Gregory, not the new numeration most unfortunately
introduced by von Soden.

manuscripts *k* and *e* and the quotations in Cyprian, which
suggest that its home was in Africa), and the Old Syriac
Version of the Gospels, then only known in the Curetonian
MS. In the Pauline Epistles there is a group of four Graeco-
Latin bilingual manuscripts which belong to this family,
and which helped to confirm its title of 'Western'. In addition certain minuscule manuscripts, of which 565 is the
most prominent, have readings of this type, though all have
been more or less influenced in the course of their tradition
by the predominant Receptus. Further (and it is this fact
which constitutes the importance of the group), all the
earliest Fathers evidently used texts more or less of this type:
Cyprian pre-eminently, in Africa, but also Justin, Marcion,
Irenaeus, and Tertullian in the West; Tatian and Aphraates
in Syria; Clement and sometimes even Origen in Egypt.

The common characteristic of 'Western' readings is a
very free variation from both the Neutral type and the
Receptus. These variations take all forms—omissions,
additions, and differences of wording, sometimes small,
sometimes considerable. A few examples may be given,
taken from the leading authorities for the group, without
at present trying to discriminate between them, or to set
out the amount of support given to each reading. In the
genealogy at the beginning of Matthew the names of
Ahaziah, Joash, and Amaziah are inserted, and the Virgin
Birth is described in several different forms of words.
After Matt. xx. 28, a long passage is inserted, beginning
'But seek ye to become great from small and small from
great', and continuing with a variant of the admonition
to take the lower place at a feast. In place of Luke vi. 5
an otherwise unrecorded incident is inserted ('On the same
day, beholding one working on the sabbath, he said unto
him, Man, if thou knowest what thou doest, blessed art
thou; but if thou knowest not, thou art accursed and a
transgressor of the law'). In v. 26 the words 'And they were
all amazed and glorified God' are omitted; also v. 39 ('No
man also having drunk old wine straightway desireth new;

for he saith, the old is better'). In ix. 55 the rebuke to the sons of Zebedee is shared by the Western text and quite late authorities. In x. 41, 42 the words 'Thou art careful and troubled about many things, but one thing is needful' are omitted. Before the Lord's Prayer in xi. 2 the Codex Bezae inserts 'Make not many words as the others do; for some think that they shall be heard in their much speaking'. In the latter part of the Gospel the narrative of the procuring of the ass for our Lord's entry into Jerusalem is much reduced; and the institution of the Lord's Supper is greatly altered. The saying from the Cross, 'Father, forgive them, for they know not what they do', is omitted by many authorities of this class; while some of them have an extraordinary addition in xxiii. 53, 'and when it [the body of our Lord] was laid there, he placed on the sepulchre a stone, which twenty men would hardly move'. In xxiv. 12 the incident of Peter's visit to the sepulchre is omitted, and in xxiv. 54 'and when he had thus spoken he showed them his hands and his feet'; while all mention of the Ascension is suppressed, only the phrase 'he departed from them' being left. In addition, throughout this Gospel there are many small verbal variations for which it is difficult to account.

In Acts the characteristic readings of the Western text are still more marked. In v. 29, in place of the usual 'Then Peter and the other apostles answered and said, We ought to obey God rather than men', we find 'Then Peter answered and said unto him, Whom ought we to obey, God or men? And he said, God'. In viii. 24 the episode of Simon Magus is closed with the words 'And he ceased not weeping much'. In x. 25 the coming of Peter to Cornelius is quite differently described: 'Now when Peter drew near to Caesarea, one of the servants ran forward and made known that he had come. And Cornelius leaping forth and coming to meet him fell down at his feet.' In xi. 2 there is a long addition: 'Peter therefore after some long time desired to go up to Jerusalem; and after speaking to the brethren and

strengthening them he went forth, and making many dis-
courses journeyed through those parts, teaching them. But
when he came to Jerusalem and made known to them the
grace of God, the brethren that were of the circumcision
contended with him.' In the narrative of Peter's deliverance
from prison a topographical detail is inserted (xii. 10), 'and
passing out they went down the seven steps'. A longer
version is given of the stirring up of the multitude against
Paul and Barnabas at Iconium (xiv. 2): 'But the leaders of
the synagogue and the chief men among the Jews raised
a persecution against the faithful and made their minds
evil affected against the brethren; but the Lord quickly
gave peace'; and further on (xiv. 5): 'And again the Jews
raised a persecution a second time with the Gentiles, and
stoned them and cast them out of the city; and they fled
and came to Lycaonia, to a certain city named Lystra'.
In the list of recommendations of the Council of Jerusalem
a new clause is added: 'And whatsoever ye would not have
done to yourselves, do it not to others.' Additional details
are also given in the narrative of the release of Paul and
Silas at Lystra (xvi. 35): 'And when it was day, the
magistrates came together into the market-place, and
calling to mind the earthquake that had taken place, they
were afraid'; and in verse 39: 'And coming with many
friends to the prison, they besought them to depart, saying,
For ourselves, we knew not that ye were just men'. In the
account of Paul's journey from Beroea to Athens a clause
is added (xvii. 15): 'But he passed by Thessaly, for he was
not permitted to preach the word to them.' The cause of
the journey of Apollos from Ephesus to Corinth (xviii. 27)
is given quite differently: 'But certain Corinthians who were
dwelling in Ephesus and hearkening to him exhorted him
to go with them to their own country; and when he con-
sented, the Ephesians wrote', &c. In xix. 1 an additional
detail is inserted: 'Now when Paul desired after his own
plan to journey to Jerusalem, the Spirit told him to turn
aside into Asia.' In xix. 9 Paul is recorded to have taught

in the school of Tyrannus 'from the fifth hour to the tenth'. On the journey from Caesarea to Jerusalem the old disciple Mnason is said to have been found at an intermediate village on the way (xxi. 16). In the account of Paul's journey as a prisoner from Jerusalem to Caesarea (xxiii. 24) a new clause is added: 'For he was afraid lest the Jews should seize Paul and slay him, and he himself might be charged with having taken a bribe.' Some additions are made to the speech of Festus (xxv. 24, 25), and the voyage along the coast of Cilicia and Pamphylia is said to have taken fifteen days (xxvii. 5). On the arrival in Rome we are informed that the centurion gave the prisoners into the keeping of the commandant of the camp; and the final words of the book are that Paul continued 'affirming and saying without hindrance that this is the Christ, the Son of God, by whom all the world will be judged'.

Now if all these well-marked divergences which have been quoted, and many more of smaller character which have not been mentioned, were uniformly found in a well-marked group of manuscripts and versions, it would be evident that we were in presence of a distinct textual family; and if these authorities were shown to be of early date and were confirmed by the quotations in the earliest Fathers, the claims of this family to respect would obviously be very strong. It is, however, of the essence of the case with which we have to deal that the evidence in support of these variants is very far from being uniform. Some of the readings are supported by most of the authorities which have been indicated as 'Western' in character, some by only a few of them in variously arranged groups, some by only one of them. Some are verbal alterations with little effect on the sense, some are additions or omissions of fact, which seem to imply revision by the author or by some person who believed himself to possess information which deserved incorporation in the original text. Collectively, they represent a large body of divergences not only from the Received Text but also from the Neutral; but whether they are entitled to be treated collectively or as a single family at all is a question which has still to be solved, and on which more will be said at a later stage.

Hort's grouping tended to present the textual problem as a contest between three well-defined families, the Receptus, the Neutral (with its rather nebulous ally the Alexandrian), and the Western. The claims of the Receptus having been disposed of, the contest resolved itself into a duel between the Neutral and the Western. As between these, Hort had no doubt as to the intrinsic superiority of the Neutral; indeed the very title he gave it, though not arising (as his opponents sometimes said) from a begging of the question, showed in what way he had, on a careful consideration of the evidence, decided the question in his own mind. Here, however, he did not meet with the same general assent among scholars as in his rejection of the Receptus; and as the dust of the controversy that arose over the Revised Version died down, the inquiries of serious criticism resolved themselves into the investigation of the character and credentials of the Neutral and Western witnesses. This has been the problem of the last forty years. It has involved an intensive study of the authorities (whether Greek manuscripts, Versions, or Patristic quotations) in which these types of text are found; and it has involved also an investigation of the conditions under which the text of the Scriptures was transmitted during the first two hundred and fifty years of the Church's life, between the dates of composition of the several books and the date at which the Received Text established its dominance in the official Church of the Empire.

These investigations have not been confined to the materials which were available at the time when Hort's classification was formed and promulgated. On the contrary, during this half-century notable additions have been made to our resources, and the problem has to be reconsidered in the light of new elements. Before proceeding to this reconsideration, it is necessary to indicate what these new elements are, what the discoveries of the last half-century (continuing down almost to yesterday) have been, and what is their bearing on the problems to be solved. It is because there is all this new evidence available that the subject can be freely rehandled without any reflection on the great scholars of the past. We stand on the foundations that they have built; but it is their foundations that have made further progress possible.

CHAPTER II

THE DISCOVERIES OF FIFTY YEARS

1. *The Sinaitic Syriac*

THE first important addition to the materials available for the textual criticism of the New Testament was made in 1892, when two Cambridge ladies, Mrs. Lewis and Mrs. Gibson, discovered and photographed in the monastery of St. Catherine at Mt. Sinai a Syriac text of the Gospels. The manuscript was palimpsest, and the Gospel text underlay a Syriac treatise dated in the year 778. On the photographs being brought home, the text was recognized by Prof. Bensly and Mr. F. C. Burkitt as belonging to the same family as the Curetonian MS., which up to that date had been the only extant representative of the Old Syriac Version. After a second expedition to Sinai in 1893, the text was published in 1894,[1] and the new find, of whose remarkable character much had been heard, was made available for the use of scholars.

On examination, it was clear that the Sinaitic MS., though undoubtedly of the same family as the Curetonian, represented that version in a somewhat earlier form. It contained many variants of the type then described as 'Western'. The most notable was in Matt. i. 16, where the Sinaitic reading is 'Joseph, to whom was betrothed Mary the Virgin, begat Jesus, who is called the Christ'. This reading was unique; the Curetonian (together with the group of Greek MSS. known as the Ferrar group or Fam. 13) has it in a modified form, 'Joseph, to whom was betrothed Mary the Virgin, who bare Jesus Christ'. The modification was no doubt due to the feeling that the reading of the Sinaitic text appeared to deny the Virgin Birth. It is clear, however, that if this was the intention of the Sinaitic

[1] A definitive edition of the Curetonian text, with a collation of the Sinaitic and an English translation, was published by Prof. Burkitt in 1904.

reading, it could not be authentic; for all the context in the Sinaitic MS. itself implies the contrary, notably the words 'when Mary his mother was espoused to Joseph, when they had not come near one to the other, she was found with child of the Holy Ghost'. Either, therefore, the reading in i. 16 is a very clumsy and incomplete attempt to eliminate the Virgin Birth, or, what is much more probable, the word 'begat' is used, as it is elsewhere in this genealogy, to indicate not literal descent but an official line of succession. In this respect the Sinaitic reading would come close to the official record, in which our Lord would of course be described as the son of Joseph. The reading therefore is interesting, though without further support it can hardly outweigh the testimony of all the other authorities; but there is no sufficient ground to regard it as heretical.

Among other important readings in the Sinaitic MS., the following may be mentioned. It agrees with ℵ and B in omitting the word 'first-born' in Matt. i. 25; in omitting 'bless them that curse you, do good to them that hurt you' and the phrase 'despitefully use you' in v. 44; and in omitting xii. 47 ('then one said unto him, Behold thy mother and thy brethren stand without, desiring to speak with thee') and xvi. 2, 3 (the passage with regard to the discerning of weather from the face of the sky); also xviii. 11 ('for the Son of Man is come to save that which was lost'). In all these cases it is very noteworthy, as showing the lack of homogeneity in the so-called 'Western' text, that D and the Old Latin version are on the other side, containing all these omitted passages, which likewise appear in the Received Text. In xix. 17, however, D and some Latin authorities join ℵ, B, and the Old Syriac in the reading 'Why askest thou me concerning the good? There is one that is good'; and again in the omission of the words 'and to be baptized with the baptism that I am baptized with' in xx. 22, 23. In xx. 28 the Sinaitic MS. is defective, so that we cannot be certain whether it contained the additional passage which occurs here in D and the Old Latin; but it is probable that it did, since it appears in the Curetonian. In xxiv. 36 it omits the words 'neither the Son', against both א B, and D and the Old Latin. In xxvii. 21, 22 it has the reading 'Jesus Barabbas', which is found also in the group of Greek minuscules known as Fam. 1; the reading was also in some Greek MSS. known to Origen. In Mark the Sinaitic agrees with א B, and the Old Latin, against D and the Vulgate, in omitting ix. 44, 46 ('where their worm dieth not', &c.), and the second half of 49 ('and every sacrifice shall be salted with salt'). In omitting the last twelve verses of St. Mark, the Sinaitic agrees with א B, but parts company with the Curetonian, which has them, as also have D and the Old Latin. In Luke vi. 5, where D has the additional incident of the man working on the Sabbath, both the Sinaitic and Curetonian are unfortunately defective; but in ix. 55 the same separation between the two Old Syriac witnesses recurs, Sinaitic agreeing with א B in omitting the words 'Ye know not what spirit ye are of', &c., while Curetonian agrees with D and the Latin versions in retaining them. So again in x. 41 Sinaitic omits, while Curetonian retains, the words 'thou art careful and troubled about many things'; in this case Sinaitic agrees with the Old Latin, but not with א B, while D has part only of the phrase ('thou art troubled'). In the Lord's Prayer (xi. 2–4) Sinaitic agrees with B in having the shortest form, omitting four words or phrases; א omits three of these, and Curetonian only one (that one being precisely the one which א retains), while D has all of them, and the Old Latin three. In the narrative of the institution of the Lord's Supper (xxii. 16–20) both Sinaitic and Curetonian have an arrangement of the verses differing from all Greek and Latin authorities. Sinaitic omits the incident of the angel in the garden and the Bloody Sweat (xxii. 43, 44), with B and the corrector of א; but Curetonian follows א, D, the Old Latin, and the great mass of authorities in retaining them. Sinaitic again differs from

Curetonian in omitting the word from the Cross, 'Father, forgive them', &c., with B, D, and some Old Latin MSS., while Curetonian agrees with ℵ and other Latin authorities in giving it. In xxiii. 48 Sinaitic and Curetonian add 'saying, Woe to us, what hath befallen us'; one Old Latin MS. has a reading almost identical, but no other authority has it. In ch. xxiv there is a series of omissions in D and the Old Latin (vv. 6, 9, 12, 36, 40), affecting the narrative of the Resurrection, but Sinaitic and Curetonian only support the last of these, omitting the words 'And when he had said this, he showed them his hands and his feet'. At the end of the Gospel (where Curetonian is defective), Sinaitic has only the phrase 'he was lifted up from them', being therefore intermediate between B, which has the full mention of the Ascension, and ℵ, D, and the Old Latin, which omit it altogether.

In John, where Curetonian is very defective, Sinaitic agrees with the Latin authorities in giving the words 'which is in heaven' in iii. 13, which are omitted by ℵ B. In iv. 9 it is allied with B and some Latin authorities in giving the phrase 'for the Jews have no dealings with the Samaritans', against ℵ, D, and other Latin authorities, which omit it. In vi. 69 it agrees with most of the Old Latin authorities and the Vulgate in reading 'Thou art the Christ, the Son of God' (omitting 'the living'), where both ℵ B and D have 'Thou art the Holy One of God'. It agrees with ℵ B and some Old Latin authorities in omitting the *pericope adulterae*, which appears in D and other Old Latin authorities. In omitting the last words of viii. 59 ('going through the midst of them and so passed by') it agrees both with ℵ B on the one hand and with D and the Old Latin on the other. In xi. 39 it has a quite singular reading, 'Lord, why are they taking away the stone?' In xviii the sequence of verses is 13, 24, 14, 15, 19–23, 16–18, so that Caiaphas appears as the questioner of our Lord instead of Annas, and the whole narrative of Peter's denial is brought together.

This list of important variants has been set out at some
length, both in order to illustrate the general character of
this early witness, and to bring out the point that there is
no clean-cut division between the so-called 'Neutral' and
'Western' authorities. In twenty-seven passages the Sinaitic
Syriac agrees 16 times with B and 12 times with א, but
only 5 times with D; with the Old Latin it shows 5 agreements and 17 disagreements, while in 5 cases the Old Latin
evidence is divided. Also in seven instances the two Old
Syriac witnesses take opposite sides. So far, therefore,
from the Old Syriac and Old Latin versions forming a
homogeneous group over against B and its supporters, the
earliest (and presumably best) Old Syriac witness sides
oftener with B than with the Latin group.

From this description and analysis it appears that the
first discovery of importance after the publication of Westcott and Hort's theory rather added to the complexity of
the problem than gave any solution of it. It was, however,
extremely valuable as broadening the base of our knowledge
of the Old Syriac version, and it constitutes an element
which must be taken into account in any ultimate solution
of the textual problem.

2. *Family 1 and Family 13.*

During the period under review intensive work has been
done on two groups of minuscule Greek manuscripts,
which it will be convenient to mention here, because of
their bearing upon subsequent discoveries. They are known
as Family 1 and Family 13, from the number of the first
manuscript in each group as it stands in the commonly
accepted catalogue of minuscule manuscripts of the Greek
New Testament. Each group consists of a number of
manuscripts which are evidently closely related, so that
they must be descended from a common ancestor of considerably earlier date than themselves; and each is noteworthy as containing a number of readings different from
the Textus Receptus. In each case there has been a good

deal of infiltration of readings from the Receptus, the amount of such infiltration differing in each manuscript; but an underlying residue of earlier readings is discernible, and scholars have devoted much pains to segregating this residue and determining its character.

The first of these groups to attract attention was that now known as Fam. 13. In 1877 W. H. Ferrar and T. K. Abbott published at Dublin a volume entitled *A Collation of Four Important Manuscripts of the Gospels*. Ferrar was the first to identify the group, and from him it has commonly been known as 'the Ferrar Group'; after his death in 1871 Prof. Abbott carried on and completed the publication. The group originally consisted of the four manuscripts numbered 13, 69, 124, and 346. 13, 124, and 346, all of the twelfth or thirteenth century, were written in Calabria, where the parent manuscript of the group must have been at that date. 69 was written, probably in England, by Emmanuel of Constantinople in the fifteenth century. Later investigation has shown traces of the same type of text in 211, 543, 713, 788, 826, 828.[1] Among the most notable readings of the group are an agreement with the Curetonian Syriac in the passage concerning the Virgin Birth (Matt. i. 16), and the omission of Matt. xvi. 2, 3, and Luke xxii. 43, 44 (the angel and the Bloody Sweat). In all these cases the family agrees with the Old Syriac, and Dr. Rendel Harris assigned it an ultimate Syriac origin; but this is one of the problems which awaits solution when the history of the Gospel text in the second and third centuries has become more clear than it is at present. Another noteworthy feature of this group is the transference of the *pericope adulterae* (John vii. 53–viii. 11) to Luke, where it follows xxi. 38. There is also a considerable number of less important variants common to this group, of which more will have to be said hereafter. So long as the group was known only as a handful of late manuscripts written in Calabria, no very great importance was attached to it;

[1] Lake, *J.T.S.* i. 117.

but subsequent discoveries called attention to it afresh, and it now appears to be taking its place in a new classification of Gospel manuscripts.

The next group to be isolated for separate examination was Fam. 1, of which an edition (with text of Cod. 1, and collation of the other members of the group) was published by Prof. Kirsopp Lake in 1902.[1] This group likewise consists of four manuscripts, Nos. 1, 118, 131, 209, of which 1 is the more important. A further interest attaches to this manuscript from the fact that it was one of those used by Erasmus in preparing the *editio princeps* of the printed Greek New Testament. It is perhaps unfortunate that he did not make it the principal basis of his text, rather than the much later and more commonplace Cod. 2; for Cod. 1 has a distinctly good text, frequently agreeing with ℵ B, and if Erasmus had followed it we should presumably have had a Textus Receptus of very superior quality, though not one so representative of the Byzantine text which dominated the Middle Ages.

Lake's analysis of the text of Fam. 1 led him in the first place to notice a phenomenon of which several other instances have since come to light, viz. that the text of Mark differs in character from that of the other three Gospels. There are now quite a number of manuscripts known in which this is the case, and it is evident that the text of Mark often escaped the revision which befell Matthew and Luke. This points to a time when the Gospels circulated in separate rolls, and when Matthew and Luke, being longer and containing more of doctrine as distinct from narrative, were more popular than Mark. They were therefore more frequently copied, their texts were more familiar, and there was more opportunity for assimilation of readings (whether intentional or unintentional) in parallel passages, and more revision to bring them into accord with officially recognized copies.

In this case Lake shows that in Mark Fam. 1 seems to form part of a larger family which includes Fam. 13 and

[1] *Cambridge Texts and Studies*, vii. 3.

the manuscripts 22, 28, 565, and 700, and which seems to have Syriac affinities. One of these (565, a fine manuscript on purple vellum at Leningrad) has a colophon, found also in some other manuscripts, stating that it was collated with early copies at Mt. Sinai which had come from Jerusalem. There is therefore some slight presumption of a Palestinian origin, but it does not go very far. In the other Gospels these relationships are not manifest. Here Fam. 1 comes nearer to ℵ B and the Old Latin than to the Syriac. For the present all that can be done is to note the facts for future reference.

The following readings may be noticed. Fam. 1 agrees with ℵ B and the Old Syriac in the omissions in Matt. i. 25, v. 44, xviii. 11, but not in those in xii. 47, xvi. 2, 3. It agrees with the same authorities and also with D in xix. 17, xx. 22, 23. In xxiv. 36 it omits 'neither the Son', with the Old Syriac; and in xxvii. 21, 22 it again agrees with the Old Syriac in the reading 'Jesus Barabbas'. In Mark it omits ix. 44, 46 with ℵ B and the Old Latin. The last twelve verses are given with a note to the effect that they were omitted in some copies and were excluded by Eusebius. In Luke ix. 55 it agrees with D, the Old Latin, and the Curetonian, against ℵ B and the Sinaitic Syriac, while in x. 41 it is with ℵ B and the Curetonian. In the Lord's Prayer Cod. 1 has the shorter version, while the other members mostly have the longer, presumably by introduction from other manuscripts. In xxii. 16–20 it has the normal order, and it shows none of the omissions which characterize the Old Latin and to some extent the Old Syriac in the latter chapters of the Gospel. In John vi. 69 it agrees with the Old Latin against both ℵ B D on the one hand and the Receptus on the other. The *pericope adulterae* is omitted in its normal place by Cod. 1, which appends it at the end of the Gospel; 209 began to omit it and had written the first words of viii. 12, but then erased these and inserted the *pericope*, presumably from another manuscript than that which the scribe was generally copying.

E

3. *The Washington Manuscript of the Gospels* (*W*)

In the winter of 1906 a group of four Biblical manuscripts on vellum was acquired from a Cairo dealer by Mr. Charles L. Freer of Detroit. Two of them contained portions of the Old Testament, two of the New. Of the Old Testament volumes, one contained the books of Deuteronomy and Joshua, and had evidently, from the numeration of the quires, originally included the entire Pentateuch. Its date appears to be of the sixth, or possibly the late fifth, century. The other was a Psalter, in a much damaged condition, which is also assigned by its editor to the fifth century, though personally I should regard it as later. Of the New Testament volumes, one contains the Gospels, the other some fragments of the Pauline Epistles. These will be described here, and the others left to be dealt with in Chapter VI. All the manuscripts were placed by Mr. Freer in the great museum containing his Oriental collection at Washington, and all have been edited, with facsimiles, by Prof. H. A. Sanders of Michigan.[1] Everything therefore was done to make them available without delay for the use of scholars.

The Gospels manuscript, which is by far the most important, is a volume of 26 quires or 374 pages, of moderate size ($8\frac{1}{4} \times 5\frac{5}{8}$ in.), with a single column of 30 lines to the page. The writing is a small, sloping uncial, quite unlike the characters of the great Biblical codices previously known. It is akin rather to the Akhmim manuscript of Enoch and to a magical papyrus in the British Museum, neither of which is certainly dated. It can hardly be later than the fifth century, and may possibly be earlier. The first quire of John is a later addition (presumably to replace a damaged quire), apparently of the seventh century. The

---

[1] *The Old Testament Manuscripts in the Freer Collection*: Part I, Deuteronomy and Joshua (1910), Part II, Psalms (1917). *The New Testament Manuscripts in the Freer Collection*: Part I, Gospels (1912), Part II, Epistles of Paul (1918). Specimen facsimiles of the Gospels and Deuteronomy in the New Palaeographical Society, Series I, pl. 201, 202.

manuscript contains the four Gospels in what is known as the Western order, viz. Matthew, John, Luke, Mark. There are two small lacunae, covering John xiv. 25–xvi. 7 and Mark xv. 13–38.

The first striking feature to catch the eye was an addition near the end of Mark. After xvi. 14 is inserted a passage which may be translated as follows:

'And they answered and said, This generation of lawlessness and faithlessness is under Satan, who doth not allow the truth of God to prevail over the unclean things of the spirits. Therefore make manifest thy righteousness. So spake they now to Christ, and Christ said unto them, The tale of the years of the dominion of Satan is fulfilled, but other terrible things draw near, and by reason of the sins of them I was delivered over unto death, that they may return to the truth and sin no more; that they may inherit the spiritual and incorruptible glory of righteousness which is in heaven.'

This passage, of which the first two sentences were known from a reference in St. Jerome (*Contra Pelag.* ii. 15), would by no one be regarded as authentic, and is not of the same class as the additions found in certain Old Latin authorities; but its occurrence called attention to the individual character of the manuscript. Further examination showed that the text was at once early, interesting, and composite. The least important part of it is Matthew and Luke from viii. 13 to the end; for here it is of the ordinary Byzantine or Received type, of which, like the Codex Alexandrinus, it is an early example. In Luke i. 1–viii. 12, and also in John v. 12 to the end (the beginning of John being contained in the supplemental quire), it falls into the 'Neutral' or Alexandrian group, of which the Vaticanus is the prime exemplar. In Mark i. 1–v. 30, on the other hand, it is closely allied to the Old Latin version; while in the rest of Mark it belongs to a different family, the identity of which had not been established at the time of its publication, and of which much will have to be said at a later stage in these lectures. For the present it must be sufficient to say that it has marked affinities with Famm. 1 and 13. Thus in the same manuscript we find different portions showing affinity to four different families of text, and these differences of allegiance do not wholly coincide with the four different Gospels. If they did, the explanation would be simple, viz. that they had been transcribed from four separate papyrus rolls, which happened to belong to different textual families. Of Matthew and John this may be true; but in Luke and Mark the scribe evidently followed different exemplars in different parts of the books. In Matthew the scribe followed one exemplar; in John and the first portion of Luke another; in the rest of Luke either a third or the first again; at the beginning of Mark a quite different one; and yet another in the remainder of that Gospel. The Washington MS. was therefore evidently produced in a library containing a varied assortment of copies of the Scriptures, or is a copy of a manuscript so produced.[1]

It will be necessary to recur to this manuscript when the time comes to consider some of the results of recent discoveries.

4. *The Washington Manuscript of the Pauline Epistles* (*I*)

Of this manuscript little need be said. It contains portions of all the Pauline Epistles from 1 Corinthians onwards, and the quire numeration proves that Acts, the Catholic Epistles, and Romans are missing at the beginning. Hebrews is placed between 2 Thessalonians and the Pastoral Epistles. The text is definitely Alexandrian in character. According to Sanders it has 67 pure Alexandrian (Neutral) readings, as against 5 Western and 15 Syrian (Byzantine); and it has 200 readings where the Alexandrian text has either Western or Syrian support against the other, as against only 9 cases where it agrees with Western and Syrian against Alexandrian. As between the members of the Alexandrian group, it tends to agree with ℵ, A, and 33 more than with B.

[1] A rather more intricate account of its genesis is given by B. H. Streeter, 'The Washington MS. of the Gospels' (*Harvard Theological Review*, April 1926).

5. *The Koridethi Gospels* (Θ)

A manuscript came to light in 1913 which, in spite of its unprepossessing appearance, has proved to have a very special interest. It is known as the Koridethi Codex, from the name of a monastery in the Caucasus region to which it formerly belonged. It is now at Tiflis. Attention was called to it by von Soden in 1906, in the *prolegomena* to his edition of the New Testament which will be mentioned presently, and it became available to scholars generally through an edition published by Beerman and Gregory in 1913. It is written in a large and extremely coarse uncial of late type, perhaps of the ninth century, though such hands are impossible to date with precision. The scribe's knowledge of Greek must have been extremely slender, but he may have been familiar with the appearance of Coptic. Dr. R. P. Blake, who has a special knowledge of Georgian manuscripts, thinks he was a member of the Georgian colony which is known to have existed in Sinai in the ninth century.

A manuscript so late in date and so rude in appearance would not seem likely to rival in interest the great uncials of the fourth and fifth centuries, and to give its name to a family. It owes this distinction to a very able study by Prof. Kirsopp Lake and Dr. R. P. Blake,[1] in which the latter describes its origin and script, and the former its text. Von Soden had associated it closely with D, but Lake shows that this is an error, and that it is not more closely allied to D than it is to B. It is, in fact, something more important than a mere satellite of either of these two manuscripts. It is closely associated with Famm. 1 and 13, and with the manuscripts 28, 565, and 700, which have been mentioned as having affinities with these families. In fact it would seem to subsume these groups into a larger family, which, until a claim to another designation is

[1] 'The Text of the Gospels and the Koridethi Codex' (*Harvard Theological Review*, July 1923).

established for it, may be described as Fam. Θ. It will thus be seen that the type of text which was first noted in the small Ferrar group has been growing in size and importance with successive discoveries during the period with which we are dealing. Its full significance will appear when we have all the evidence before us. Meanwhile it must suffice to say that the discovery of the Koridethi MS. is one of the more significant events in the history of the period with which we are dealing.

6. *Other Vellum Manuscripts*

Briefer mention must suffice of a number of other Greek manuscripts on vellum which have been either discovered or first fully examined since 1881. The most noteworthy are a group of manuscripts on purple vellum which, though discovered at different times and in different places, are all of the same period (probably sixth century) and are closely related in character and appearance. One of them, at Rossano, known as Σ or 042, was discovered by Gebhardt and Harnack in 1879, and published by the former in 1883. It contains Matthew and Mark and is ornamented with a remarkable series of paintings. In 1886 the Abbé Batiffol published a similar manuscript (but without paintings) which had been for many centuries at Berat in Albania. This also contains only Matthew and Mark; it is known as Φ or 043. Ten years later 182 leaves of another purple manuscript, which had been seen in Cappadocia so far back as 1883, were acquired by the Tsar, and proved on examination to be part of a manuscript of which thirty-three leaves were already known at Patmos, six in the Vatican, four in the British Museum, and two at Vienna. One other leaf has since been identified at Genoa. Taken together, the manuscript (which appears to have been broken up by Crusaders in the twelfth century) amounts to about half of the complete volume. All Gospels are represented in it, but Luke and John more fully than the other two. The text was edited by Mr. H. S. Cronin in

1899. Its distinctive letter is N. Finally, in 1900, M. Omont published forty-three leaves, written in gold letters on purple vellum, and containing five illustrations, which had been brought from Sinope in the previous year by a French naval officer. It contains parts of the latter half of Matthew, and is known as O.

Textually as well as in outward appearance, these four manuscripts form a closely connected group. N and Σ in particular are practically sister manuscripts. Their text is substantially that of the Textus Receptus, but in an early stage, so that they form a link between A and the fully developed Byzantine text. Φ, however, is peculiar in having the long addition after Matt. xx. 28, which is also found in D.

More interesting textually, though later in date (eighth or ninth century), is the manuscript known as Ψ or 044, seen at Mt. Athos by Gregory in 1886, but first fully examined by Lake in 1899. It agrees with L (the contemporary Codex Regius in Paris) in giving the shorter alternative ending to St. Mark, in addition to the ordinary last twelve verses; and in general character it also falls into the same class with L in showing a considerable amount of agreement with the Vaticanus. It contains the Gospels from Mark ix. 5 onwards, the Acts, and Epistles. According to Lake (*Journal of Theological Studies*, 1900), its text is especially good in Mark.

Some other uncial manuscripts have come to light since 1881, but they need no special mention. Of minuscule manuscripts several hundreds have been added to the list, chiefly from the monasteries in the East, notably Athos, Sinai, and Jerusalem. Many of these were examined for von Soden's edition (to be mentioned in the next chapter); and more has been, and is still being, done by Lake and his colleagues. Most of them, as was to be expected, offer only the Textus Receptus; but here and there some have been found that contain relics of an earlier text. Nothing of fundamental importance has yet emerged, or perhaps is likely to emerge, from this source; but some assistance may be obtained from them, in conjunction with the other authorities that have been mentioned, in reconstructing those earlier families of text which precede the Textus Receptus, and with which we are principally concerned.

7. *Papyrus Fragments*

Among the multitudinous discoveries of Greek papyri in Egypt during the last fifty years a considerable number of fragments of Biblical manuscripts have come to light. The seventeen volumes of the *Oxyrhynchus Papyri* alone contain fifty such fragments, of which thirty belong to the New Testament; and many others lie scattered in the publications of various institutions. A complete catalogue of them would be very helpful to Biblical students.[1] For the most part they are very small; and this is particularly the case with regard to the New Testament. The largest is a papyrus from Oxyrhynchus (P. Oxy. 657, now Brit. Mus. pap. 1532), probably to be assigned to the late fourth century, containing portions of Hebrews (ii. 14–v. 5, x. 8–xi. 13, xi. 28–xii. 17), written on the back of an epitome of Livy. This is of some importance, in view of the failure of the Vaticanus after Heb. ix. 14.

Three others deserve special mention. One is a leaf of a papyrus codex of Matthew, in the library of Michigan University,[2] containing Matt. xxvi. 19–52, in a hand which may be assigned to the end of the fourth century. The text does not fall wholly into any of the recognized categories. It has readings in common with the Neutral and Western texts, and with the family, to be described hereafter, which is known as Caesarean. Two others, one at Michigan and one at Rome, contain portions of the latter part of Acts,

[1] Such a catalogue has in fact been made by the Rev. P. L. Hedley, who has been good enough to inform me that it contains 157 items from the New Testament, and 174 from the Old. These figures include vellum fragments and ostraka as well as papyri. It is hoped that this catalogue may be published before long.

[2] Edited by Sanders, *Harvard Theological Review*, xix. 215 (1926).

and present very interesting peculiarities. The Michigan papyrus[1] contains Acts xviii. 27–xix. 6, xix. 12–16, and is assigned by its editor to the first half of the third century, which is probably too early. It has very decided 'Western' affinities, agreeing notably with the Codex Bezae in xix. 1 and 14, where that manuscript differs markedly from the Vaticanus and is supported only by the margin of the Harklean Syriac. It also has minor agreements with D and a few peculiar readings of its own, but only a few agreements with the Vaticanus. It is thus definitely an adherent of the Western type in its most advanced style.

The Roman papyrus[2] is a mutilated leaf of a codex, attributed to the latter part of the third or beginning of the fourth century, containing Acts xxiii. 11–17, 23–9. In that short space it contains about a dozen readings differing markedly from the ordinary text. Some of them have Latin or Syriac support (Cod. Bezae is defective here), while some are wholly new; but all are characteristically Western. This papyrus therefore definitely ranges itself with that at Michigan as evidence for the existence in Egypt, not later than the latter part of the third century, of texts which are not merely non-Neutral but are definitely Western in the full sense in which that term is applied to the Codex Bezae and the African Old Latin.

The other New Testament papyri that have hitherto come to light are so small that it is often impossible to decide their character, and in no case is it possible for that character to be strongly marked. Singly, therefore, they have almost no importance, but collectively they have some value as giving us a glimpse into the condition of the New Testament text in Egypt in the early centuries. They range in date from the third century to the seventh. Those which are of the fifth century or later can be dismissed from consideration, since we have ampler evidence elsewhere

[1] Sanders, ibid. xx. 1 (1927).
[2] Edited by Vitelli as no. 1165 of the *Papiri della Società Italiana*, with assistance from Mgr. Mercati.

F

for this period; but those which can be assigned to the third or fourth century deserve careful scrutiny. There are a considerable number of these. Unfortunately no complete inventory of them has yet been published; but among thirty New Testament papyri included in the Oxyrhynchus volumes up to date, twenty-one are of this period.

The questions to which we look for an answer from these fragments are naturally, Do they, or do they not, confirm the superiority of the Vaticanus over all others? Do they show at least that the Vaticanus type of text was dominant in Egypt? Or do they give any support to Hort's hypothesis of a non-Vaticanus text also existing in Egypt, which he designates as 'Alexandrian'? Or do they prove the existence of the so-called 'Western' text in Egypt in these early centuries? In short, do they throw any light on the problems that are troubling us?

The answer to all these questions except the last is in the negative; and this fact is itself the answer, not altogether negligible in value, to the last question. The evidence of each single fragment is by itself so slight that no conclusion could be drawn from it; but the significant fact which emerges from the study of all of them is that they will not fall cleanly and systematically into any of Hort's categories. As was to be expected, they habitually support the earlier manuscripts as against the Textus Receptus; but as between the earlier manuscripts themselves their favours are divided. Of hardly any can it be said that they distinctly support the Vaticanus against other authorities, though several are rather of this character; of none except the two fragments of Acts above mentioned can it be said that it is definitely 'Western'.[1] In general it has to be said that, so far as they go (and that is not very far), they seem to reveal a period in which the New Testament text had not crystallized into families, but was still in a state of flux. This suggestion,

---

[1] P.S.I. (*Papiri della Società Italiana*) 2 + 124, which has some verses of Luke xxii, is rather of this character.

too uncertain if it rested only on these small fragments, may be of some use eventually in connexion with other evidence.

8. *The Coptic Versions*

Since a large proportion of the new material that has become available in the last fifty years is due to discoveries in Egypt, it is natural that the Coptic versions have benefited by them to a considerable extent. Only the most important of these need be mentioned here. It so happens that several substantial Coptic Biblical manuscripts have come to light. Perhaps the finest of all is a complete Psalter in the Sahidic version, now in the British Museum (Or. 5000), a splendid papyrus codex of 156 leaves measuring $11\frac{3}{4} \times 8\frac{1}{2}$ inches. The dates of Coptic manuscripts are notoriously difficult to decide, but this may be of the seventh century. Another (Or. 5984), originally containing the Sapiential books, consists of sixty-two leaves of even larger size ($14\frac{1}{4} \times 10\frac{1}{2}$ in.). More important is a papyrus codex acquired by the British Museum in 1911 (Or. 7594), containing a curious combination of books, Deuteronomy, Jonah, and Acts, in a Sahidic text.[1] The addition of a note at the end of it in a cursive script, which can be assigned with some confidence (on the strength of dated Greek papyri) to about the middle of the fourth century, gives a *terminus ante quem* to the Biblical text, which must belong to the first half of that century; and this is confirmed by the presence in the binding of several scraps of Greek papyri, datable about A.D. 300. For Acts, therefore, we have an almost complete Sahidic manuscript of about the same date as the Vaticanus. The Old Testament books will be further referred to in the final chapter.

Another important discovery was made in 1923 by Mr. Guy Brunton, excavating near Assiut on behalf of Sir Flinders Petrie's British School of Archaeology in Egypt. This was a papyrus codex containing nearly the whole of

[1] Edited by Budge, *Coptic Biblical Texts in the Dialect of Upper Egypt* (1912): a collation printed privately by Sir H. Thompson (1913).

John (ii. 12–xx. 20), in a hand more comparable with Greek scripts than is usual in Coptic manuscripts, and apparently assignable to the third quarter of the fourth century.[1] The dialect is between Achmimic and Sahidic, and therefore presumably represents the Achmimic-Sahidic version (for textually they appear to be the same) in a very early form. It shows a considerable number of variations from all other Sahidic texts; its editor enumerates 110, in 63 of which it differs from both Sahidic and Bohairic, while in no less than 40 it agrees with the Bohairic against the Sahidic. This is important evidence in favour of the presence of early elements in the Bohairic, or of an early date for the whole version. As compared with the Greek uncials, it shows decidedly stronger affinities with B and W than with א.

An important group of Sahidic manuscripts, apparently of the eighth or ninth century (one is dated A.D. 893) was discovered in 1910 and acquired by Mr. J. Pierpont Morgan, in whose library they now are. Besides some books of the Old Testament, which will be mentioned later, they include one copy of the Gospels, two of the Pauline Epistles, and one of the Catholic Epistles. Photographic facsimiles of these have been published, and a brief check-list (1919), but the texts have not been printed.[2] The collection also includes a Gospel Lectionary, and a Bohairic copy of the Gospels (mutilated) of about the twelfth century.

The Sahidic version has gained more than the Bohairic from the discoveries of recent years, since its origin and circulation were in Upper Egypt, where buried papyri are preserved by the dryness of the climate, while the home of the Bohairic was in the moister climate of Lower Egypt. The materials, consisting mainly of small fragments, but

---

[1] Edited by Sir Herbert Thompson, *The Gospel of St. John according to the earliest Coptic Manuscript* (1924).

[2] A collation of the Pauline Epistles is given as an appendix in Horner's edition of the Sahidic New Testament, in which the date is said to be not earlier than the eleventh century.

covering collectively the whole New Testament, have been made easily accessible in Mr. G. Horner's edition; but the discovery of manuscripts of complete books greatly facilitates an estimate of its character. In the main the effect has been to emphasize its adherence to the textual type represented by B ℵ, to which the Bohairic essentially belongs. It has a considerable sprinkling of readings of a different type, and used therefore to be regarded as belonging rather to the 'Western' group. It does not have, however, the more extravagant features of that group, and it may be questioned whether these readings are not rather the residuum of the early texts of the second and third century, which are not Western more than they are Eastern or Southern, and the history and character of which constitute the main problem of textual criticism to-day.[1]

Some additional Coptic evidence will be mentioned when I come to deal with the latest discovery of Biblical manuscripts known as the Chester Beatty Papyri; but the description of these will be more conveniently reserved until some account has been given of the developments of textual theory which preceded them; for the interest of the new material lies in the light which it throws on the conclusions at which textual critics had been arriving.

9. *The Latin Versions*

The principal additions to our materials in respect of the Syriac and Coptic versions have been mentioned above (§§1 and 8). In regard to the Latin versions there is nothing material to add in the way of new witnesses, but a good deal of editorial work has been in progress. The most important (though unfortunately very imperfect) manuscript of the Old Latin, *k*, was exhaustively edited by Wordsworth and Sanday in 1886; but Hort already was

---

[1] Out of 209 readings in Acts, amounting in length to a στίχος or nearly so, which are printed in heavier type by Prof. A. C. Clark in his recent edition as specially characteristic of the Western text, Sahidic support is quoted for 25.

aware of its importance as containing a text identical with that used by Cyprian, and therefore to be located in Africa. Others of the Old Latin manuscripts have been edited or re-edited, especially by Belsheim and in the Oxford series of *Old Latin Biblical Texts*; so that the evidence for this version is more fully available than before.

Meanwhile the text of the Vulgate is in course of being established on a sure foundation by the great Oxford edition of Wordsworth and White, of which the Gospels appeared in successive parts in 1889–98 and Acts in 1905, Romans (after the death of Bishop Wordsworth in 1911) in 1913, 1 Corinthians in 1922, and 2 Corinthians in 1926.

It will be seen therefore that our knowledge of all the principal versions has been greatly extended during the past fifty years, while some of the less-known versions, notably the Armenian and Georgian, are proving themselves to possess a previously unsuspected importance.

10. *The Fathers*

As was indicated above, the quotations from the New Testament in the writings of the early Fathers are of crucial importance in fixing both the date and place of various types of text. Decisive use of this testimony was made by Hort; yet in his time the study of the Fathers was hampered by want of reliable editions of them. Quotations of Scriptural passages were especially liable to be modified by scribes in accordance with the form of Biblical text known to them, which of course was of the prevalent Byzantine pattern; and little had been done to rectify this by the critical study of the best manuscripts of the Fathers. Within the last half-century, however, two great series have been in progress, the Berlin Corpus of the Greek Fathers and the Vienna Corpus of the Latin, which are gradually removing this difficulty and enabling scholars to use this material without the fear that they may be deducing their conclusions from insecure evidence.

In this chapter the attempt has been made to indicate

very summarily (and it is to be feared imperfectly) the principal additions made to our textual material during the last fifty years. Such evidence provides a most searching test of the theories of Westcott and Hort; for none of it was known to them, and their theories must stand or fall according as the new witnesses are found compatible with them or not. The evidence is early in date, of varied geographical provenance, diversified in character. It is only regrettable that, for lack of an up-to-date critical apparatus embodying its results, students have to search far and wide to bring it together and make use of it. In the next chapter something will be said of the developments of textual theory to which it has so far led.

CHAPTER III

DEVELOPMENTS IN TEXTUAL THEORY

1. *Von Soden's Edition*

ONE result of the stimulus given to textual criticism by Westcott and Hort and the Revised Version, and by the constantly increasing influx of new material, was to create a demand for a new critical edition of the New Testament, to replace that of Tischendorf, which (in the final form of its eighth edition) had appeared as long ago as 1869–72. Not only had the mass of materials greatly increased, but the standard of accuracy and minuteness in collation had risen, and photography had brought manuscripts far more easily within the reach of students. A new and amply subsidized edition was accordingly undertaken in Germany, under the direction of Prof. H. von Soden, which after many years of preparation appeared in successive parts in the course of the years 1902–13. This was an event of the first magnitude, since the new edition comprised a complete overhaul of the manuscript material, a multitude of new collations, a rehandling of the history of the New Testament text, and finally a new text, based upon the textual theories at which the author had arrived.

Von Soden's work was a very great achievement, and the mind sometimes recoils at the thought of the immense amount of meticulous labour entailed on the editor and his assistants. It has added greatly to the mass of material available for scholars, especially in respect of the collations of minuscule manuscripts. If the collations are not always found to be accurate, that, it is to be feared, is the almost inevitable result of human frailty when handling enormous masses of details. More distressing, and a very serious handicap to the utility of the edition, is the fact that von Soden had the unhappy idea of renumbering all the manuscripts. His object was by the designation of each manuscript to indicate something of its date and contents. Thus one set of numbers is allotted to manuscripts earlier than the tenth century, another to those of the tenth century, and others to those of succeeding centuries; with modifications according as the manuscript contains the entire New Testament, the Gospels, the Acts, the Epistles, or the Apocalypse. The result is a complication which makes the edition, while possibly manageable by a student handling it every day, extraordinarily difficult for occasional reference. Moreover, it is very disconcerting to find the familiar nomenclature of the most important manuscripts replaced by new names; to have to recognize B as δ1 and A as δ4. If the experiment had been successful, every student would have had to bear in mind a double name for each leading manuscript, or would find all previous textual work unintelligible. The annoyance of scholars at the change, and their reluctance to use it, were increased by the reflection that the compensating gain claimed for it was negligible and illusory. It is only before A.D. 1000 (or even earlier) that the precise century of a manuscript matters much, and here the system gave no help; after A.D. 1000 the dating of Greek minuscules is by no means assured, so that the information given may be wrong, and in any case is unimportant.

The danger of finding the old nomenclature superseded by this new and cumbrous system was averted by the action of C. R. Gregory, who (after consultation with all the principal textual students in Europe and America) produced a revised form of Tischendorf's list, which has received general acceptance; and it is not necessary to refer further to it here.[1] The importance of von Soden's edition lies in his attempt to reclassify the authorities (especially the Greek manuscripts, for he pays comparatively little attention to the versions), and to substitute a new classification

[1] Descriptions of von Soden's system will be found in an article in the *Church Quarterly Review* (Oct. 1914), or in my *Handbook to the Textual Criticism of the New Testament*, 2nd ed., London, 1912, pp. 52–5.

and new nomenclature for the 'Neutral', 'Alexandrian', 'Western', and 'Syrian' of Hort, and other variants of these by Hort's predecessors and successors. His classification is as follows. The whole body of authorities is divided into three main groups, designated by the letters K, H, and I. K (Κοινή) represents the main mass of later manuscripts, named by Hort Syrian, by others Antiochian or Byzantine or Textus Receptus. H (Hesychian) includes the group of which the Vaticanus is the head, and is practically equivalent to Hort's 'Neutral'. Von Soden regards this group as the result of a recension by the Alexandrian scholar Hesychius, who is known to have produced an edition of the Septuagint, but of whose connexion with the New Testament the evidence is in fact extremely shadowy. Finally, I (Jerusalem) is a new group, supposed to have originated at Jerusalem, which includes such authorities as D, the Old Latin, Old Syriac, Famm. 1 and 13, &c.

Of these groups H is comparatively simple. It includes only about fifty manuscripts, mostly imperfect, and for most purposes is represented by B ℵ, or their common ancestor, which is denoted by the symbol δ^{1-2}. B is regarded as the best representative of the group, but has been influenced by both I and K^1. I has a large number of subdivisions, which for the greater bewilderment of scholars are not designated by the parent letter but by various other symbols, such as H^r (Fam. 13), J (Fam. 1), Φ, K^a (a group which is regarded as an I text revised in the direction of K, which might equally be said of all the others), Π (the group of purple manuscripts described in the last chapter), and so on. D is assigned to a group known as I^a, which is a mixture of I and K^1. K naturally has a still larger number of subdivisions, of which K^1 is the earliest, while K^x is the dominant text from the tenth or eleventh century onwards. The Codex Alexandrinus is placed in K^a, a group which has been influenced by H, and which itself has many subdivisions. In all, there appear to be twelve main subdivisions of I, and sixteen of K, while in each subdivision the extent to which each manuscript is a full adherent varies indefinitely.

The most valuable part of von Soden's prolegomena is probably his analysis of the K group; but since this group is the one of least value for the recovery of the original text, the total effect is hardly commensurate with the labour bestowed on it. Still, it may serve as a starting-point for the inquiries of others. The treatment of the I group, which von Soden regards as his special discovery, is the least satisfactory of all. It is vitiated by the inclusion of the Codex Bezae (which he declares to be the most brilliant confirmation of the existence of the I group) and the Old Latin in one group with Famm. 1 and 13 and their allies. In this connexion he was unlucky in the fact that the discoveries of W and Θ, which so greatly strengthened this group, were made too late to be of any use to him.

Having divided his authorities into these three main groups, the next task is to find the common basis, I-H-K, which lies behind them. K is believed to have originated in Syria in the fourth century, and is perhaps due to Lucian (though here again, while we know that Lucian produced an edition of the Septuagint, there is no evidence that he also edited the New Testament). H is the text used by Athanasius and Cyril of Alexandria; it evidently originated in Egypt, and is attributed to Hesychius. I is the text used by Cyril of Jerusalem, and is probably due to Eusebius of Caesarea. The common ancestor I-H-K must be dated before Origen, i.e. round about A.D. 200 at latest, and was used (though not exclusively) by Origen, and subsequently by the later Egyptian Fathers and by Jerome. Even with I-H-K, if we can recover it to our satisfaction, we have not reached the end (or the beginning) of variations. For these von Soden finds a prime cause of disturbance in Tatian's Diatessaron, which he believes to have been originally written in Greek, and to have had a widespread and deleterious influence on the Old Latin and Old Syriac versions and the texts used by the early

Fathers. If the variations due to this cause could be eliminated, we should not be far, in von Soden's opinion, from the original verity.

This theory of the influence of Tatian, and his reconstruction of the I group of manuscripts, are von Soden's most novel contributions to textual history; and it cannot be said that either has made a favourable impression on scholars in general.[1] On the whole, while fully recognizing that there is much material in his volumes of which others can make use, it is difficult to avoid the conclusion that his renumeration of the manuscripts is a calamity, his classification unsatisfactory, his theory with regard to the influence of Tatian unproven (and indeed he devotes little space to it), and his resultant text no advance on its predecessors. The formation of a new critical apparatus still remains an urgent desideratum, and the veil has still to be lifted from the early stages in the textual history of the New Testament.

2. *The Caesarean Text*

Throughout the years that followed the publication of Westcott and Hort's edition, a small band of scholars were constantly at work on the problem of textual criticism. This activity was perhaps greatest in England and America. It took the form of articles and reviews, and sometimes of collations of particular manuscripts, which it would be superfluous to enumerate or describe in detail; but special tribute is due to the work of Rendel Harris, F. C. Burkitt, C. H. Turner, and A. Souter in England, and Kirsopp Lake (himself first trained in England), J. H. Ropes, and H. C. Hoskier in America. At first the main trend of discussion was in the direction of emphasizing the importance of the Western element as against the Neutral. The Old Latin version received much attention from Wordsworth and

---

[1] Some drastic criticisms on both may be found in Lake's pamphlet, *Professor H. von Soden's Treatment of the Text of the Gospels* (Edinburgh, 1908).

White (in preparation for their great edition of the Vulgate), Sanday, Rendel Harris, Turner, and Burkitt. The Old Syriac was brought into prominence by the discovery of the Sinaitic palimpsest, and Burkitt's competence as an Orientalist has given him special qualifications for handling both the main branches of the 'Western' text. From another angle interest was concentrated on this text by Blass's theory of a double edition of both Luke and Acts (in which books the most remarkable 'Western' variations occur) by Luke himself, the 'Neutral' text being in fact Luke's earlier edition of the Gospel and his later edition of Acts, while the 'Western' text gives the later edition of the Gospel and the earlier of Acts; a theory worked out with characteristic ingenuity by its author, but which hardly stands the test of close scrutiny.[1] Thus for a time the 'Western' text held the centre of the stage, and there was a tendency to hold that the original text must be sought here rather than in the 'Neutral' family.

Meanwhile, a good deal of work was being done by Lake, Hoskier, and others in examining and collating the manuscript material which had previously been unknown or inadequately examined; and this line of study was reinforced by the discovery of the Freer MSS. and the Koridethi Gospels. It was from this side that the next great advance in textual theory was to come. As stated above, Lake in 1913, following up his previous work on Codex 1 and its allies, showed that the Koridethi Gospels (Θ) in Mark formed a family with the smaller groups known as Fam. 1 and Fam. 13 and with the minuscule manuscripts 28, 565, and 700. All these manuscripts had been more or less affected by revision in the direction of the current Byzantine text; but if their Byzantine readings were eliminated, they were shown to present a common text agreeing neither with the 'Neutral' nor the 'Western' types as

---

[1] My own analysis of it, for what it is worth, is given in my *Handbook to the Textual Criticism of the New Testament* (2nd ed.), ch. viii, § 4.

represented respectively by B and D, but about equidis-
tant between them. As to the place of origin of this recension, Lake's colleague, Prof. R. P. Blake, starting from the
Georgian character of the script of Θ, suggested Sinai,
where there was a Georgian colony, and which was in
touch with Jerusalem on the one hand and Egypt on the
other.

In 1924 Canon B. H. Streeter, in his remarkable book
The Four Gospels, carried the matter much farther. First
he produced evidence to show that the conclusions at
which Lake had arrived in respect of Mark held good also
of the other Gospels, so that we have here a distinctive
text with a claim to stand by itself alongside the other main
textual groups. Next he showed that this family has
marked affinities with the Old Syriac, both in additions
to the Textus Receptus which it shares with D and the
Old Latin against B, and in omissions which it shares with
B against D and the Old Latin. The Greek text underlying
the Old Syriac was therefore nearer to the ancestor of Θ
than to either B or D; but they are not identical, for in a
considerable number of readings Θ supports the Armenian
version against the Syriac; while Blake has shown ground
for the belief that the Georgian version is an even closer
relative of Fam. Θ. At this stage, after rejecting the suggestion that this text might be connected with Eusebius
(to whom, it will be remembered, von Soden attributes
his I text) by showing that the text of Eusebius, though
often agreeing with Θ, is far more strongly tinctured with
D, he was led to investigate the text of Origen, and thereby
to make a remarkable discovery, which deserves to be
noted as an epoch in Biblical criticism. From an examination of Origen's commentaries on Matthew and John and
his *Exhortation to Martyrdom* (in all of which extensive
quotations occur from all four Gospels), he arrived at the
conclusion that in the first ten books of the *Commentary on
John* Origen used a manuscript of Mark of the same type
as B ℵ, while in the remaining books of this work and in

the *Commentary on Matthew* and the *Exhortation* he used a manuscript of the same type as Θ. With regard to Matthew, the result was substantially the same, though some of the quotations (as so often happens in the case of the more popularly used Gospels, Matthew and Luke) have been assimilated to the Byzantine texts in our manuscripts of Origen. For John, throughout his commentary on that book, he seems to have used a manuscript of Alexandrian type, while for Luke he changed at some point to the Θ type.

Now the significance of this change of type lies in the fact that Origen wrote the first five books of his *Commentary on John* at Alexandria, while the rest of it, together with the other two works, were written at Caesarea in Palestine, to which place he removed in A.D. 231. The conclusion to which this points obviously is that, whereas at Alexandria Origen had at his disposal manuscripts of the Alexandrian (i.e. 'Neutral') type (and probably brought away with him the copy of John on which he was commenting), at Caesarea he found manuscripts of the type represented by Θ and its allies. In other words, *the text of Fam. Θ may rightly be called the Caesarean text.*

There are from time to time books which mark a definite turning-point in the studies to which they relate. Streeter's *Four Gospels* is such a work in connexion with the textual criticism of the New Testament. Utilizing the work of others over a period of many years past, and adding thereto valuable contributions of his own, he has made good a definite addition to our knowledge, and established a fresh starting-place for further progress. Henceforward the Caesarean text has an assured place in textual criticism.

Streeter had thus said the first and most important word about the Caesarean text, but he had not said the last. Lake, who had started the whole inquiry by his investigation of Codex 1, and who had actually at one time suggested a connexion between it and Caesarea, returned again to the subject, and with the assistance of his colleagues Blake and Mrs. New undertook an edition of the Caesarean text of Mark, and as a foretaste of it produced in 1928 an elaborate study of the subject.[1] In this he added to the members of the group the Freer Gospels (W), which is plainly Caesarean in the greater part of Mark, and a newly published seventh-century fragment at Berlin (P. 13416), with a fuller study of the Georgian evidence. But the great advance made was in respect of Origen's use of the Caesarean text. He pointed out that whereas Streeter had argued that Origen used an Alexandrian text of Mark in the first ten books of his *Commentary on John*, only the first five of these (as we know from his own statement quoted by Eusebius) were written at Alexandria, and in these five books the evidence as to Origen's text of Mark is extremely small, and may be interpreted at least as much as indicating the use of a Caesarean text as of an Alexandrian. In books 6–10 he unquestionably used an Alexandrian text; but the significant point is that he used it at Caesarea, not at Alexandria. In the remaining books he seems to have used an Alexandrian text when quoting from the greater part of Mark, but a Caesarean text for the latter part (after about the middle of ch. xii); and in all his subsequent writings his text is definitely Caesarean.

The result of this closer analysis of the evidence is that Streeter's contention that Origen used an Alexandrian text at Alexandria and a Caesarean at Caesarea must be modified. It appears on the contrary that, according to the slight evidence available, he may have used a Caesarean text before his departure from Alexandria; that he certainly used an Alexandrian text at first after his arrival at Caesarea; but that before long he reverted to a Caesarean text, and used it thenceforward for the rest of his life. The possibilities therefore remain open (1) that the Caesarean text originated in Alexandria, (2) that Origen himself brought it to Caesarea and established it there. These

[1] 'The Caesarean Text of the Gospel of Mark' (*Harvard Theological Review*, xxi. 207–404).

possibilities must be borne in mind for consideration with the later evidence which still has to be described, and with any that may yet come to light in the future.

Further conclusions of Lake and his colleagues are that the Caesarean text was used by Eusebius (which Streeter denied), and that it is most fully represented in Mark (to which Gospel alone their inquiry relates) by Θ, 565, 700, and the Georgian version, though the other members of the group occasionally contribute readings which have been lost in these. The Georgian version in particular, especially in its earliest representative (the Adysh MS., written in 987) turns out to be highly important in this connexion; and since it is certain that the Georgian version was a translation from the Armenian, it would appear that when it was made there existed an Old Armenian version which, to a greater extent than any existing Armenian manuscript, was a relatively pure representative of the Caesarean text. Whether the Armenian version was made direct from the Greek or from the Syriac is a debatable point. Macler maintains the former; but Blake gives strong reasons for believing that it was originally made (as is *a priori* more probable) from the Syriac, and was subsequently revised from Greek manuscripts, first of the Alexandrian and subsequently of the Byzantine type. A Caesarean text also appears to underlie the Palestinian Syriac lectionaries, and this again appears to point to the existence of the Caesarean text in a Syriac form.

As a result, therefore, of the investigations of Lake and Streeter von Soden's classification of his I family must, it would seem, be abandoned. The Western group (D and the Old Latin) must be definitely separated from the group, headed by Θ, which has been isolated as the text of Caesarea. For the constitution of this text there is now a considerable quantity of material, and the edition of Mark, on which Lake and his colleagues are now engaged, will be awaited with much interest. There will still remain the question of the origin, Egyptian or otherwise, of this type of text, and its bearings on the general history of the New Testament text in the second and third centuries. Additional material for the consideration of these problems, and perhaps some light on their solution, are provided by the very recent discoveries which still remain to be described.

CHAPTER IV

THE CHESTER BEATTY PAPYRI

SO far an attempt has been made to describe the positions at which textual knowledge and criticism had arrived at the moment when the greatest discovery of new Biblical manuscripts, at least since the Freer collection, and possibly since the Codex Sinaiticus, was made. This consisted of a group of papyri from Egypt, acquired from dealers by Mr. A. Chester Beatty, of which the first public announcement was made in *The Times* of 19 November 1931.

The discovery consisted of portions of twelve distinct manuscripts, of which eleven contained portions of the Greek Bible, while the twelfth included an apocryphal book and a Christian homily. All are imperfect, and portions of some of them are known to be in other hands, while it is far from impossible that other portions still remain with the natives who discovered them. The place of discovery has not been revealed, but there is reason to believe that it was in the district of the Fayum; and from the nature of the collection it is fairly clear that it must come from the ruins of a Christian church or monastery.

All the manuscripts are on papyrus, and all are in codex form; and all are early in date. The earliest appears to be as early as the second century; the latest is not later than the fifth. Eight of them contain portions of the Old Testament, three of the New. The following is the complete list, in which precedence is given to the New Testament manuscripts, since that is the intended order of publication. The official numbers assigned to them in the New Testament by von Dobschutz and in the Old Testament by Rahlfs, who keep what are generally accepted as the official registers of the manuscripts of the Greek Bible, are attached to them. Since the original announcement some additional fragments have come to light, which accounts for some differences in the descriptions now to be given. These were acquired by the University of Michigan, but the authorities of that University, with great courtesy and liberality, ceded them to Mr. Chester Beatty, to whom the major part of the manuscripts in question belonged.

I. Gospels and Acts: 30 leaves (all more or less mutilated) containing portions of Matt. xx. 24–32, xxi. 13–19, xxv. 41–xxvi. 3, 6–10, 19–33; Mark iv. 36–ix. 31, xi. 27–33, xii. 1–28; Luke vi. 31–41, 45–vii. 17, ix. 26–xiv. 33; John x. 7–xi. 57; Acts iv. 27–xvii. 17. 3rd cent., perhaps in the first half [P⁴⁵].

II. Pauline Epistles: 10 leaves, of which 8 are in conjugate pairs, containing Rom. v. 17–vi. 14, viii. 15–35, ix. 22–xi. 33; Phil. iv. 14–23; Col. i. 1–iii. 11; and small fragments of Col. iv. 16–18; 1 Thess. i. 1, 9, 10, ii. 1–3, v. 5–9, 23–8. Probably 3rd cent. [P⁴⁶].

III. Revelation: 10 leaves, containing Rev. ix. 10–xvii. 2. Probably late 3rd cent. [P⁴⁷].

IV. Genesis: 44 leaves, containing Gen. ix. 1–xiv. 13, xvii. 7–xlii. 2, with considerable mutilations. 4th cent. [961].

V. Genesis: 22 leaves, containing Gen. xxiv. 13–xxv. 21, xxxi. 50–xxxv. 16, xxxix. 4–19, xli. 9–xlvi. 33, with mutilations. Written in a document hand of the latter part of the 3rd cent. [962].

VI. Numbers and Deuteronomy: substantial portions of 33 leaves, with smaller portions of 22 more, and a large number of fragments, many of which have not yet been placed. The leaves as at present reconstituted contain Num. v. 12–viii. 19, and portions of xiii. 4–6, 17, 18, xxii. 11–38, xxv. 18–xxxvi. 13; Deut. i. 20–vii. 19, and portions of ix–xii, xviii, xxviii–xxxiv. Apparently first half of 2nd cent. [963].

VII. Isaiah: 27 leaves, very imperfect, containing portions of Isa. viii. 18, ix. 2, xi. 5–xix. 13, xlii. 1, xlv. 5, liv. 4–lx. 22. Fragments of xvii. 5–7, 9–12, liv. 14–17, lv. 3–6 are in private hands. A few notes have been written in the margins, some of them Coptic. Probably first half of 3rd cent. [965].

VIII. Jeremiah: one imperfect leaf, containing Jer. iv. 30–v. 1, v. 9–13. Probably late 2nd or 3rd cent. [966].

IX. Ezekiel and Esther: 16 leaves in 8 conjoint pairs, containing Ezek. xi. 25–xvii. 21; Esther ii. 20–viii. 6. The two books are written in different hands, apparently of the latter part of the 3rd cent. [967].

X. Daniel: 13 leaves, containing Dan. iii. 72–vi. 18, vii. 1–viii. 27, with large lacunae, since about two-fifths of the height of each leaf is lost. The text is of the original Septuagint, not the version of Theodotion. Probably first half of 3rd cent. [968].

XI. Ecclesiasticus: one leaf and part of a second, containing Ecclus. xxxvi. 28–xxxvii. 22, xlvi. 6–11, 16–xlvii. 2. Probably 4th cent. [964].

XII. Enoch and a homily: 8 leaves in the Chester Beatty collection and 6 in the possession of the University of Michigan, containing Enoch 97–107 and a Christian homily (unidentified). 4th or 5th cent.

So large an addition, not of mere fragments but (except the Jeremiah) of substantial portions of manuscripts, to the list of extant Biblical papyri is obviously an event of great importance. In the first place they make a notable extension backwards in date of the tradition of the text of the Greek Bible. Hitherto there has been nothing except small fragments earlier than the period represented by the Vaticanus and Sinaiticus, that is, about the middle of the fourth century, which marks the beginning of the vellum period of palaeography. Now we have three substantial manuscripts of the New Testament, covering, to a greater or less extent, ten books, which can be assigned with some confidence to the third century, and eight of the Old Testament, covering nine books, of which one is as early as the second century, and five not later than the third. The full value of this additional evidence cannot be realized until scholars have had time to scrutinize it with care, but it can hardly fail to enlarge materially our comprehension of the history of the Bible text.

It will be convenient to take first a minor point, of bibliographical character, which nevertheless is of some interest. The Chester Beatty papyri confirm decisively the recognition of a fact for which evidence has been accumulating for some time past, namely, the early use of the codex form of book by the Christian community. It is matter of common knowledge that the accepted form of book in the classical periods of Greece and Rome was the papyrus roll. It is equally well established that from the fourth century onwards the vellum codex took the foremost place in book production. The history of the transition from papyrus to vellum, and from the roll to the codex, or modern book form, has been obscure. Discoveries in Egypt have revealed the existence of an intermediate form of book, the papyrus codex, and there have for some time past been indications that this form was especially favoured by the Christian community; but its exact relations to the earlier and later forms have been uncertain. Now the situation is beginning to clear up. Statistics based upon the discoveries in Egypt (whence alone evidence, other than literary allusions, is derivable) show the papyrus roll in universal use for pagan literature up to the end of the second century, and in overwhelming preponderance throughout the third.[1] For Christian writings there was no evidence which could be assigned with any confidence to the second century; but in the third the examples of the papyrus codex outnumbered those of the roll, and the vellum codex began to appear. The Chester Beatty papyri now fully confirm the use of the papyrus codex in the Christian community in the third century, and also (if the dating of the Numbers-Deuteronomy manuscript be accepted) carry it back into the second, and even perhaps to the first half of that century. It is true that this particular manuscript belongs to the Old Testament, and *may* have been produced in Jewish rather than Christian surroundings; but in view of the deep-rooted tradition of the use by the Jews of the roll for the Book of the Law, this is not very probable,[2] and in any case we must now be prepared to admit the possibility of the use of the codex for the New Testament books in the second century.

[1] The statistics are given in my book, *Books and Readers in Ancient Greece and Rome* (Oxford, 1932).

[2] A special argument against the Jewish origin of the manuscript may be found in the use of the contracted forms $\overline{\text{ιης}}$, $\overline{\text{ιην}}$, &c., for the name of Joshua, a practice not likely to be followed by any but a Christian scribe, to whom 'Ιησοῦς was familiar as a sacred name, and as such usually represented by an abbreviation, as in the case of θεός, κύριος, &c.

A consequence follows, which, though bibliographical in character, is of high importance for New Testament criticism. The normal length of a papyrus roll, which rarely exceeded 35 feet, would not suffice for more than one of the longer books, Matthew, Luke, or Acts. So long, therefore, as the roll was the normal form of book, each of the Gospels must have occupied a separate roll, and would have circulated separately. A given Christian community might only have possessed one or two Gospels; and those Gospels which were the most popular would have been more frequently copied, and therefore more exposed to the corruption which comes from copying, than the others. It is thus easy to understand why Mark, which was less popular than the fuller narratives of Matthew and Luke, has often been handed down in a more primitive form than the others. Hitherto it has been reasonable to suppose that this state of affairs lasted throughout the third century, and that possibly the four Gospels were never united in a single volume until the final victory of the vellum codex. It is now clear that this was not so. We now have an actual example of a codex of the third century containing all four Gospels and the Acts, and another which contained all the Pauline Epistles (with the exception of the Pastorals). More than this, if the codex form was in use among the Christians of the second century, they may have already been accustomed to see the four Gospels in a single book, and so have come to regard them as a unity, on a different level of authority from any other narrative of the life of our Lord. This would make it easier to understand how Irenaeus, for example, can already argue that the number four is essentially appropriate, shown by various analogies to be in accordance with God's method of dealing with the world. It is now evident that, while the Gospels no doubt continued to circulate also in separate rolls, they certainly were sometimes combined in codex form in the third century, and possibly also in the second.

To come now to consider the character of the three New

Testament manuscripts in the Chester Beatty collection (reserving the Old Testament manuscripts for treatment in a separate chapter). The most important is unquestionably that of the Gospels and Acts. All five books are represented, and there is no doubt that all formed part of a single codex. The hand is the same throughout, and the remains of a page numeration on two pages of Acts clinch the proof. Calculation shows that approximately 220 pages would be required to contain the five books, and the two numbered pages, which occur in chapters xiv and xvii of Acts, are numbered 193 and 199. The hand is small and clear, without being calligraphic, leaning to the right, with rounded curves and no marked excrescences either in height or width. The original size of each leaf was about 10×8 inches, the columns of writing measuring about $7\frac{1}{2} \times 6\frac{1}{4}$ inches, with normally 39 lines of text to the page. The writing being small, there is an appreciable quantity of text even on quite moderate-sized fragments.

The sixty pages of which portions survive are thus distributed. Only four pages belong to Matthew, and the remains of these are so small as to be almost negligible, though they contain a few interesting readings. Mark is represented by twelve pages, of which six are of substantial size, though far from complete. Luke is in better case, there being fourteen pages, of which all but two have the complete width of the column of writing, though some lines are imperfect or lost at the top and bottom of each page. Of John there are two pages complete in width and about two-thirds complete in height, and two with only half their width. Acts is the most fully represented of all, having portions of twenty-six pages, though none of them approaches in completeness the best of Luke and John. It will be seen therefore that while Matthew is hardly represented at all, of all the other books enough is preserved to enable the character of the text to be determined. There are very many passages not preserved in which we should have been glad to be able to quote the authority of this very early witness; but there is ample material for ascertaining the textual character of the manuscript and its place in the textual history of the New Testament.

One result which has emerged from the intensive study of manuscripts during the past generation, and to which reference has previously been made in these lectures, is that the text of Mark not infrequently shows a different character from that of the other Gospels. Not a few manuscripts, which have quite ordinary Byzantine texts in the other three Gospels, preserve in Mark readings of a different and evidently early character. The reason, as indicated above, probably is that Mark, being the shortest of the Gospels and containing less of the teaching of our Lord, was less read and less copied than the others, and consequently suffered less both from ordinary scribal errors and from the assimilation of readings to which the Synoptic books are liable. Consequently it is not surprising to find that the relations between this papyrus and other early manuscripts are somewhat different in the different Gospels. In Mark the important fact emerges at once that the papyrus clearly ranges itself with the Caesarean group. The manuscript with which it shows the closest affinity is the Freer MS. at Washington (W). Next to this comes Fam. 13, then Cod. 565, Fam. 1, and Θ, and then Cod. 700. With these definitely Caesarean authorities it obviously stands in a much closer relation than with any others. With regard to the other main witnesses, it is slightly closer to A than to D, and definitely less close to B and א. If the Caesarean text is to be regarded (as suggested by Lake) as intermediate between Neutral and Western, the text as shown in the papyrus is in this Gospel nearer to the Western wing, but quite clearly does not fall into the Western group.

In Luke the relationships work out differently. The Caesarean text for this Gospel has been much less fully established than for Mark, and the known witnesses for it are fewer. W, for the greater part of the Gospel (including the whole of the portion preserved in the Chester Beatty papyrus), has a Byzantine text, and Θ also is more Byzantine here than in Mark. Whether it is fair to assume that the papyrus (which is too early to have been affected by Byzantine texts) here represents the Caesarean family, it would be premature to affirm definitely until it has been compared with the quotations in Origen and Eusebius; but the possibility is to be borne in mind. The manuscripts with which it shows the highest proportion of agreements are B and its colleague L. Next to these comes D (if the more marked divergences of D in this Gospel are left out of account), then א, Fam. 13, Fam. 1, and W; while Θ and A are more distant. There is a rather large number of agreements with D in small groups, somewhat larger than with B L א, and much larger than with any other manuscript.

In the comparatively small portion of John contained in the papyrus the proportions are again somewhat altered. There is not much to choose, in respect of agreements, between the three families. D, Θ, B, and א (in that order) show the highest figures of agreement, and Fam. 1 and W follow very closely. Fam. 13, curiously enough, is much farther away, with no better figures than A and the Textus Receptus. Agreements with D in small groups are again relatively high, but only in respect of minor variations.

Finally, in Acts (where it will be remembered that A joins the Neutral group) the papyrus agrees more with א A B than with D, and has none of the more marked variants of the latter.[1] In all the books it has a considerable number of readings which do not occur in any of the leading uncials, but these (when they are not merely

---

[1] Prof. A. C. Clark's important edition of Acts appeared when the present volume was in the final stage of proof revision, and could not be taken into account. But it may be observed that of 77 readings printed by him in heavier type as specially characteristic of the 'Western' text, as to which the evidence of the papyrus is available, not one is supported by the papyrus.

scribal errors) relate almost exclusively to minor details, such as the order of words.

The net result is that the papyrus, while not agreeing wholly with any of the main families as otherwise known to us, is definitely Caesarean in Mark; and if we cannot affirm the same positively with regard to the other Gospels, that may be because in them the Caesarean text is less well known to us. It will be highly interesting to compare the papyrus with the quotations in Origen and Eusebius from these Gospels. For the moment all that can be said is that in Luke and John it stands about intermediate between Neutral and Western, but without any of the more marked peculiarities of the latter. Its agreements with D are rather in respect of the minor variants found in Western authorities. This suggests the need for discrimination between readings which have hitherto been lumped together under the designation 'Western', as to which more will have to be said.

Special importance attaches to the Chester Beatty papyrus by reason of its age. Not only does it carry back the evidence for the text of Gospels and Acts, in a substantial form, by perhaps as much as a century, but it throws light on the highly important period during which the various families of the text were taking shape. By its age it is necessarily free from any suspicion of Byzantine revision; and it shows us, as existing at a local centre in Egypt, a text free from the marked divergences characteristic of the Western text. It is therefore a witness to the substantial integrity of our textual tradition, while making an invaluable contribution to our knowledge of the early stages of that tradition.

It will be convenient to reserve for the next chapter the final summing-up of the position in which this new witness, in combination with those previously mentioned, seems to leave the problems of textual criticism, and to close this chapter with the description of the other New Testament manuscripts in the Chester Beatty collection.

The second Chester Beatty papyrus contains the Pauline Epistles, and again gives us for the first time proof that these writings were known as early as the third century in a collected form which was impossible so long as the papyrus roll was the only vehicle of publication. Of the ten leaves in the Chester Beatty collection, eight are joined together in pairs, showing that they form part of a single quire. The other two can be shown to have been originally joined together, but are now separate. The first four (together with the first detached leaf) contain part of the Epistle to the Romans, and six of the pages bear numbers ranging from 20 to 29. The other four, with the fragments of the other detached leaf, contain the end of Philippians, the beginning and end of Colossians, and some small scraps of 1 Thessalonians; and the first page bears the number 17[0].[1] Hence it is evident that the manuscript is an example of an early form of papyrus codex, in which a large number of leaves were combined in a single quire. In this case a simple mathematical calculation shows that the codex must have consisted of from 100 to 104 leaves, formed of 50 to 52 sheets of papyrus folded once in the middle. Seven leaves are missing at the beginning (and therefore also at the end), and from 70 to 74 leaves in the middle. The seven leaves at the beginning contained Rom. i. 1– v. 17; the 70–4 in the middle whatever intervened between Rom. xi. 36 and Phil. iv. 14; and the seven at the end whatever followed 1 Thess. v. 28. Calculation shows that the space in the middle can best be accounted for on the supposition that it included Hebrews in addition to 1 and 2 Corinthians, Galatians, and Ephesians. For such a position of Hebrews there is confirmation in the Sahidic version, which places this Epistle between 2 Corinthians and Galatians, while the section-numbering in the Vaticanus shows that in some ancestor of that manuscript it followed Galatians.

[1] Since the last figure is lost, the numbers 170, 172, 174, 176, and 178 are all possible.

The seven leaves which must have followed that which contains part of 1 Thessalonians would have been more than sufficient to contain the conclusion of that Epistle and the whole of 2 Thessalonians. It would be enough to hold 1 Timothy, but not the rest of the Pastoral Epistles; and it is perhaps most probable that some pages were left blank at the end.

With regard to the text of the Pauline Epistles, all that can be said at present is that the manuscript is certainly not of the Byzantine type, and is definitely nearer to the אּ A B group, and especially to B, than to the Western group D F G. It shows, however, several agreements with F G in small groups, though fewer than with B. The order of agreement after B is A, אּ, C, D, F G, with the Textus Receptus a long way behind. There are a considerable number of singular readings, but none of much importance.

The manuscript is written in a flowing, rather calligraphic hand, which can safely be assigned to the third century, and may be early in it. It is totally unlike the hand of the Gospels manuscript.

The third of the New Testament manuscripts in the Chester Beatty collection is composed of ten leaves of papyrus, measuring when complete about $9\frac{1}{2} \times 5\frac{1}{2}$ inches, and containing the middle third of the book of Revelation, from ix. 10 to xvii. 2. From one to four lines are lost from the top of each page; otherwise the text is complete and continuous. The hand is of medium size, rough and irregular, with no pretensions to style or beauty, but generally correct. It is plainly of the Roman period of palaeography, and may be assigned to the third century and probably to the latter part of it.

The text of Revelation falls into three main families, though there are minor subdivisions which have been exhaustively studied by Mr. Hoskier. These three are (1) the Textus Receptus, which in this book is mainly, but not wholly, the text of the minuscule Codex 1, a twelfth- or thirteenth-century manuscript of good quality used by

Erasmus; (2) a group of about forty minuscules headed by the eighth-century uncial **046**,[1] representing a definite revision; (3) the four earlier uncials ℵ A C P. These four uncials do not, however, form a uniform group. They have no near common ancestor, but are four distinct representatives of an early text which had already diverged to a considerable extent. The Chester Beatty papyrus now makes a fifth member of this group. It is definitely more in agreement with ℵ A C P than with **046**, and still more than with the Textus Receptus. It does not, however, range itself very closely with any one of the four, showing in every case more disagreements than agreements. It has the highest proportion of agreements with ℵ and C, next with P, and slightly less with A. The variations of text in the Apocalypse are not of great importance, but the papyrus now takes rank as the earliest authority for the book.

In addition to these Greek manuscripts, Mr. Chester Beatty also acquired at a rather earlier date a group of Coptic papyri of certain books of the Bible. There were five manuscripts in all in this find, of which three were purchased by Mr. Chester Beatty, and two by the University of Michigan. An inscription in them shows that they belonged to the monastery of Apa Jeremias, near Sakkara, and as they were found with gold coins of Justinian which do not appear to have been long in use, they may probably be assigned to the sixth century; a conclusion quite consistent with the palaeographical evidence. Mr. Chester Beatty's portion of the find has been edited by Sir Herbert Thompson.[2] One manuscript contains the Pauline Epistles and the Gospel of St. John; another, the same Gospel and

[1] Formerly known as B₂, but it is better to avoid the use of this letter, since it suggests a connexion with the great Codex Vaticanus, which is defective in this book, and with which this manuscript has nothing to do.

[2] *The Coptic Version of the Acts of the Apostles and the Pauline Epistles in the Sahidic Dialect* (Cambridge, 1931).

the Acts; and the third Psalms 1–50, with an intruded quire containing Matt. i.1–ii. 1. One of the Michigan MSS. contains the remainder of the Psalter; the contents of the other have not been announced.

In text, these manuscripts generally support the Codex Vaticanus, especially in the Pauline Epistles; but there are traces of a Western element, especially in Acts. Prof. Burkitt, in reviewing Sir H. Thompson's book,[1] argues that this implies that the original basis of the version was of Western type, most of the specifically Western character having been removed by correction to bring it into accord with the Neutral type, dominant in Egypt. The opposite process, however, also seems conceivable, since a scribe might have been tempted to introduce Western readings which appeared to him to be attractive; or, perhaps more probably (since there is no obvious reason for the selection of these particular readings, which are in no case of the more striking class of Western readings), they may perhaps be explained as belonging to the category of unassorted early non-Neutral readings, the existence of which is certain, but whose connexion with the specifically Western type of text appears questionable.[2]

[1] *Journal of Theological Studies*, July 1932.
[2] See above, p. 37.

CHAPTER V

RESULTS AND SPECULATIONS

WE are now in a position to sum up the results of the work and the discoveries of the last fifty years, and to try to form some judgement as to the present position of the textual problems presented by the New Testament. At first sight the general impression is one rather of dis-integration than of greater certainty. Westcott and Hort's analysis of the textual material seemed to present a fairly clear-cut result: (1) the large mass of later authorities, which can be eliminated as representing a secondary text ('Syrian', otherwise called Byzantine or Antiochian or Textus Receptus); (2) a small group of authorities, among which the Codex Vaticanus (B) stands out pre-eminently, containing a text which has the internal marks of purity and originality ('Neutral', otherwise called Egyptian or Alexandrian or Hesychian); (3) a rather miscellaneous band of authorities, principally Latin or Syriac, of early date, but presenting a text which has the marks of extensive editorial alteration ('Western'). Hort's fourth class ('Alex-andrian') can for our present purpose be ignored, since it is only a sub-family of the second, formed to cover those readings which, though appearing in Egyptian authorities, are not accepted as part of the 'Neutral' text, but are regarded as due to minor stylistic modifications of it.

These conclusions, if universally accepted, would have greatly simplified the textual problem. As between families, the Neutral reading would almost always be preferred; and in determining the Neutral reading in any particular case, an editor would hardly go wrong in accepting the evidence of B, except in cases of obvious scribal errors. There were a few modifications of this absolute faith in B, which need not be taken into account here. The criticism of the last fifty years has, however, greatly blurred the edges of these clear-cut results. The absolute authority of B (though not its general excellence) has been questioned, and the authority of its principal supporter, ℵ, has been still more challenged. It has been shown that texts circulated extensively in Egypt which did not conform to the 'Neutral' pattern. A new family, called 'Caesarean', has been brought to light, and has been shown to possess very strong claims to consideration. The 'Western' family, which never presented much appearance of coherence, has been still further disintegrated, while the number of witnesses possessing 'Western' characteristics to a greater or less extent has been increased. Finally, the mass of later authorities has been analysed, principally by von Soden, and certain main groups of it more or less successfully isolated.

What conclusions can be drawn from this reshuffling of the evidence? Perhaps the most convenient method will be to take each group separately, and see how it stands in the light of our present knowledge.

Of all the terms that have been applied to the common or received text, 'Byzantine' seems the most unobjectionable, because it begs no question as to its origin. It merely affirms that it is the type of text which eventually came to be adopted throughout the Byzantine Church and Empire, and of this there is no doubt. Since there is now no question among scholars as to its generally secondary character, the examination of its origin and history has receded in importance. Nevertheless, just because it became the Bible of the Greek Church in general, and thereby the text in which, after the invention of printing, the Greek New Testament was known for nearly four hundred years, it must always be an object of interest, and any light that can be thrown on its origin would be very welcome. No one has yet succeeded in attributing it with any certainty to any place or person. Indeed all the evidence tends to show that it is the result of a long-continued process rather than of a deliberate revision. Von Soden's classification assigns its finally dominant form (K^x) to the tenth or eleventh century, but this is preceded by several earlier

K

stages. Its earliest use appears to be by Chrysostom, which would place its origin in the fourth century, and since it is also found in the Antiochene commentary on the Gospels, von Soden (like Hort) regards Antioch as its probable place of origin. He would even go farther, and attribute it (as Hort had tentatively suggested before him) to the hand of Lucian, who worked at Antioch at the beginning of the fourth century (d. A.D. 311); but for this attribution there is very slight evidence. Lucian is known to have produced an edition of the Septuagint, and if he had also produced an edition of the New Testament it is extremely unlikely that this should not have been recorded. Moreover, if Lucian or any other scholar was responsible for any revision of the New Testament text of this character, it can only have been the beginning, or an intermediate stage, in a long process, not the end. No manuscript of a date approaching that of Lucian shows the Byzantine text in its full form. The earliest which can be assigned to this family is A (in the Gospels, not in the other books); and this is not by any means a pure K or Byzantine text. The Peshitto Syriac also, which Burkitt has shown to be the work of Rabbula in the first quarter of the fifth century, has the Byzantine text in a relatively early form. The group K^1, which von Soden regards as the best form of K, is found in several manuscripts, of which the oldest is of the eighth century; and this is followed by K^x in the tenth or eleventh century, and K^r (a revision for liturgical purposes) in the twelfth. We see therefore the process of revision in several stages from the fourth to the twelfth century, and there is no proof that anything was done in the fourth century of a decisively different character.

The main characteristics of the Byzantine text are a smoothing away of verbal roughnesses, small additions intended to make the meaning clearer, and assimilation of parallel passages in different Gospels. It is a natural process in a text so familiar and so repeatedly copied as the Gospels. Either consciously, to make his text clearer,

a scribe might add pronouns, substitute familiar for unfamiliar turns of expression, or harmonize the narrative of
an event in one Gospel with that given in another; or
unconsciously his memory might lead him to write the
more familiar phrase instead of the less. Further, if a scribe
had two or more manuscripts before him, he would be
much more likely to select the easier or the more familiar
phrase than to apply the canons of scientific textual
criticism; and so the process of contamination of the
original text would go on.

For the purpose, therefore, of recovering the original
text, the Byzantine type in its later forms can be ignored
entirely, and even in its earlier forms is of comparatively
little value. Such value as it has is for comparison with the
earlier types, and for the light that it may throw on the
handling of the sacred books in the early ages of the Church.
In its several stages it represents the treatment of the Bible
text by the Church throughout its history, until it was
stereotyped by the invention of printing.

The Neutral family remains practically unchanged in
its content since Hort's time. No considerable new manuscript has come to light which can be assigned to it. At
most one or two small papyrus fragments may possibly
have belonged to manuscripts of this class; though it is
dangerous to come to any such conclusion on the evidence
of two or three readings. The family therefore is still
mainly represented by B ℵ in the Gospels, reinforced by
A C in the other books. Next to these come the fragmentary
T and the minuscules 81 and 33, followed by L and the
very imperfect R and Z, with sporadic support from other
sources. The Bohairic version belongs predominantly to
this family; and according to Wordsworth and White the
manuscripts used by Jerome in the formation of his Vulgate
text were also of this type, though the revision of the
previously existing Latin version was so incomplete that the
Vulgate is far from presenting a fully Neutral text.

The Neutral family, therefore, is in itself little changed

by the discoveries of fifty years. But what of its character? Is it really 'neutral', i.e. a fairly good representative of the original text, uncontaminated by serious corruption, either deliberate or accidental? Or is it the result of editorial revision, whether by Hesychius (as suggested by Bousset and accepted by von Soden) or another? Does it hold to-day the same dominant position as it held in the eyes of Tischendorf and Hort?

It is clear that some abatement must be made from Hort's claims. Although this type of text is obviously Egyptian in origin and home, it is not possible to maintain that Egypt had preserved an uncorrupted form of text, of which B is a characteristic example. The papyri of earlier date than B, fragmentary as they are, suffice to show that the B text did not prevail universally in Egypt; and the Sahidic version, though it has strong affinities with B, tells the same tale. It is evident that in Egypt, as in other parts of the world, texts existed in the third century which were not of the B type. B may still represent a tradition which has come down with little contamination from the earliest times; but, if so, the stream ran in a narrow channel, and did not water, like the Nile, the whole land of Egypt.

Since B and ℵ are so far alike that they must have had a common ancestor, and so far different that their common ancestor cannot have been a very near one, the origin of the Neutral text is at any rate carried back well into the third century. This in itself is an objection to attributing it to Hesychius, who is believed to have laboured about A.D. 300–10; and the attribution, which rests on a single passage of Jerome, has in any case little to support it, since Jerome's own language seems inconsistent with it.[1] The

---

[1] Jerome's words are (*Ep. ad Damasum*): 'Praetermitto eos codices quos a Luciano et Hesychio nuncupatos paucorum hominum adserit perversa contentio.' If Jerome was himself using manuscripts of the Hesychian revision, he could not have spoken so slightingly of it; and if he was referring to any other manuscripts, what becomes of his evidence of an Hesychian authorship for the B or Neutral type of text?

real question to be decided is, Is this text the product of editorial revision or of exceptionally pure transmission? Westcott and Hort maintained that it showed none of the characteristics of editorial handling, and Weiss, as the result of an entirely independent examination, came to the same conclusion. He finds many scribal errors in B, but regards it as the only manuscript which has escaped deliberate revision. Here the question must be left for the moment, until the remaining families have been examined.

The Caesarean family is a new accession to the textual phenomena that have to be dealt with, and the most important new element in the problem. As described above, it is formed out of two new discoveries, the Koridethi MS. (Θ) and the Washington MS. (W), together with the two previously known groups of minuscule manuscripts designated as Fam. 1 and Fam. 13, and certain other minuscules, of which 28, 565, and 700 are the most prominent. To these has now been added an important reinforcement in the shape of the Chester Beatty papyrus (P[45]), which is the earliest in date of them all. In textual character the family holds a position intermediate between the Neutral family headed by B and that type of the Western family which is headed by D; and it derives special importance from its connexion with Origen and Eusebius and the school of Caesarea.

If Streeter's original conclusion, that Origen's use of this type of text is found only in works produced after his migration to Caesarea, had held good, it would have been natural to attribute the origin of the type to editorial revision, possibly by Origen himself, during his residence at Caesarea. Lake's correction of Streeter's argument cast serious doubt on this conclusion, making it probable that Origen used a 'Caesarean' text while still in Alexandria, and an 'Alexandrian' text on his first arrival in Caesarea, though he subsequently reverted definitely to the Caesarean type. This seems to suggest that the best manuscripts at Caesarea prior to Origen's arrival were of the Alexandrian type, and that he made use of them for a time; but that he eventually satisfied himself of the superiority of the Caesarean type, which he had known in Egypt, and which he had perhaps himself brought to Caesarea or procured to be sent there.

The weak point in this argument, as presented by Lake, was the small amount of evidence as to the text used by Origen in Egypt. So far as it went, it pointed to a Caesarean type; but it was so small in amount as to make the conclusion precarious. The Chester Beatty papyrus strongly reinforces it, by proving the existence in Egypt of the Caesarean type of text at a date either contemporary with Origen or at any rate not much later. Once again, then, a clean-cut picture has become blurred on further investigation. Instead of finding one type of text prevalent in Egypt and one in Palestine, we find the Caesarean text pre-existing in Egypt, and the Alexandrian preceding the Caesarean at Caesarea. The Caesarean text is shown to be Caesarean by adoption rather than by birth, and Egypt is shown to be the home, not of one uniform type of text but of several.

It should be added by way of warning that these conclusions must be taken as provisional rather than assured. The examination of the Caesarean text and the assessment of its character are still in their early stages. Work has been concentrated mainly upon Mark, and the other Gospels have been as yet only lightly touched. In particular, the Chester Beatty papyrus has not yet been published, and the statements made about it depend solely on my own examination of it in the course of transcribing it and preparing it for the press. These results will need to be checked and extended by better-equipped scholars over a longer range of time.

For our present purpose the main point is to note that we have now in the Caesarean family, whatever its origin and character, a well-established entity, comparable in date with the Neutral group, and with no extravagances to arouse suspicions. Its identification deprives von Soden's I group of most of its value; indeed it may be said to take its place, setting free the Latin or Western elements which von Soden incongruously included in the group to fall back into their own proper surroundings, which have now to be investigated.

The so-called 'Western' family has been at all times the storm-centre of textual criticism. It challenges attention by the number and boldness of its departures alike from the familiar Textus Receptus and from the Neutral text which Hort exalted to the chair of authority. It claimed attention by the early date of the authorities cited in its support, which included the earliest versions (Old Latin and Old Syriac) and most of the earliest Fathers. Since Hort's time it has received reinforcement in the discovery of the Sinaitic Syriac, besides a dropping fire of isolated readings and pieces of evidence. On the other hand, it has been subjected to a good deal of disintegrating criticism.

The difficulty in dealing with the 'Western' family is to know what the term really connotes. It is best known by certain striking additions and omissions in the text, especially in Luke and Acts, and by a marked independence of phraseology in the general course of the narrative. Divergences so marked as these have a character of their own, which has to be accounted for. But the term 'Western' is also applied to a number of smaller variants of a less provocative character which also appear in the same early authorities. In this connotation 'Western' comes almost to mean any reading which is early in date but which does not find a place in the Neutral family. I believe that textual criticism has no more urgent need than to take the whole *corpus* of early non-Neutral readings, to investigate their character, and to endeavour to trace them to their sources, which I am much disposed to believe will be found to be not one but many. In this task the evidence even of the smaller finds from Egypt may play a useful part; while the Chester Beatty papyri offer the invaluable assistance of a body of evidence going back to the third century and casting light back on an even earlier period.

Some progress has already been made with this inquiry. Prof. Burkitt showed, many years ago, that the larger additions to the Gospel text are to be found mainly in the oldest form of the Old Latin, that which is represented by the African group of authorities, the manuscripts *k* and *e* and the quotations of Cyprian. The smaller additions appear principally in the European Latin group, the manuscripts *a b* and their allies; while the Syriac authorities by no means always agree with the Latin. An example, taken from Luke v, where variations of this type are somewhat plentiful, will make the facts clearer:

Luke v. 5, 6. χαλάσω τὰ δίκτυα. καὶ τοῦτο ποιήσαντες B *a b*: οὐ μὴ παρακούσομαι· καὶ εὐθὺς χαλάσαντες τὰ δίκτυα D *e* Syr[s].

7. συλλαβέσθαι B: βοηθεῖν D Lat.

8. λέγων B Syr[s].; + παρακαλῶ D *c e f* Syr[p].

10. 11. ὁμοίως δὲ καὶ Ἰάκωβον καὶ Ἰωάννην υἱοὺς Ζεβεδαίου, οἳ ἦσαν κοινωνοὶ τῷ Σίμωνι. καὶ εἶπεν πρὸς τὸν Σίμωνα Ἰησοῦς· μὴ φοβοῦ· ἀπὸ τοῦ νῦν ἀνθρώπους ἔσῃ ζωγρῶν. καὶ καταγαγόντες τὰ πλοῖα ἐπὶ τὴν γήν, ἀφέντες πάντα ἠκολούθησαν αὐτῷ B Syr.: ὁμοίως δὲ καὶ Ἰάκωβος καὶ Ἰωάννης οἱ υἱοὶ Ζεβεδαίου κ.τ.λ. א *a b c ff*[2]: ἦσαν δὲ κοινωνοὶ αὐτοῦ Ἰάκωβος καὶ Ἰωάννης υἱοὶ Ζεβεδαίου. ὁ δὲ εἶπεν αὐτοῖς· δεῦτε καὶ μὴ γίνεσθε ἁλιεῖς ἰχθύων· ποιήσω γὰρ ὑμᾶς ἁλιεῖς ἀνθρώπων. οἱ δὲ ἀκούσαντες πάντα κατέλειψαν ἐπὶ τῆς γῆς καὶ ἠκολούθησαν αὐτῷ D *e*.

12. πεσὼν ἐπὶ πρόσωπον ἐδεήθη αὐτοῦ B *a b* Syr.: ἔπεσεν ἐπὶ πρόσωπον D *e*.

13. ἡ λέπρα ἀπῆλθεν ἀπ' αὐτοῦ B *a b* Syr.: ἐκαθαρίσθη D *e* (cf. Mark i. 42).

14. εἰς μαρτύριον αὐτοῖς B *e* Syr.: ἵνα εἰς μαρτύριον ᾖ ὑμῖν τοῦτο D *a b c ff*[2], &c. D adds (from Mark i. 45) ὁ δὲ ἐξελθὼν ἤρξατο κηρύσσειν καὶ διαφημίζειν τὸν λόγον ὥστε μηκέτι δύνασθαι αὐτὸν φανερῶς εἰς πόλιν εἰσελθεῖν, ἀλλ' ἔξω ἦν ἐν ἐρημοῖς τόποις, καὶ συνήρχοντο πρὸς αὐτόν. καὶ ἦλθεν πάλιν εἰς Καφαρναούμ.

17. καὶ αὐτὸς ἦν διδάσκων, καὶ ἦσαν καθήμενοι Φαρισαῖοι καὶ οἱ νομοδιδάσκαλοι οἳ ἦσαν ἐληλυθότες B Syr. *a b*, &c.: αὐτοῦ διδάσκοντος συνελθεῖν τοὺς Φαρισαίους καὶ νομοδιδασκάλους· ἦσαν δὲ συνεληλυθότες D *c e*. D (alone) omits καὶ Ἰερουσαλήμ· καὶ δύναμις κυρίου ἦν.

19. ἀναβάντες ἐπὶ τὸ Δῶμα Διὰ τῶν κεράμων καθῆκαν αὐτὸν σὺν τῷ κλινιΔίῳ B Syr.: ἀνέβησαν ἐπὶ τὸ Δῶμα καὶ ἀποστεγάσαντες τοὺς κεράμους ὅπου ἦν καθῆκαν τὸν κράβαττον σὺν τῷ παραλυτικῷ D (paraphrasing Mark ii. 4).

25. ἐφ’ ὃ κατέκειτο B Syrˢ.: τὴν κλείνην D e Syrᵖ.: κλινίΔιον ἐφ’ ᾧ κατέκειτο a b c.

26. καὶ ἔκστασις ἔλαβεν ἅπαντας καὶ ἐΔόξαζον τὸν θεόν B Syr.: om. D e fam. 13.

27. καὶ μετὰ ταῦτα ἐξῆλθεν καὶ ἐθεάσατο τελώνην ὀνόματι Λευείν B Syr., &c.: καὶ ἐλθὼν πάλιν παρὰ τὴν θάλασσαν τὸν ἐπακολουθοῦντα αὐτῷ ὄχλον ἐΔίΔασκεν· καὶ παράγων εἶΔεν Λευὶ τὸν τοῦ Ἀλφαίου D (paraphrasing Mark ii. 13, 14).

29. οἳ ἦσαν μετ’ αὐτοῦ κατακείμενοι B: ἀνακειμένων D e.

30. καὶ ἁμαρτωλῶν B Lat.: om. C D.

33. οἱ Δὲ σοὶ ἐσθίουσιν καὶ πίνουσιν B: οἱ Δὲ μαθηταί σου ἐσθ. καὶ πίν. b c f ff²: οἱ Δὲ μαθ. σου οὐΔὲν τούτων ποιοῦσιν D e.

34. μὴ Δύνασθε τοὺς υἱοὺς τοῦ νυμφῶνος, ἐν ᾧ ὁ νυμφίος μετ’ αὐτῶν ἐστιν, ποιῆσαι νηστεῦσαι B f l q: μὴ Δύνανται οἱ υἱοὶ τοῦ νυμ. ἐν ᾧ . . . ἐστιν, νηστεύειν ℵ a b c ff²: μὴ Δύνανται οἱ υἱοὶ τοῦ νυμ., ἐφ’ ὅσον ἔχουσιν τὸν νυμφίον μεθ’ ἑαυτῶν, νηστεύειν D e.

38. βλητέον B: βάλλουσιν ℵ D a b c e. A C D Lat. add. καὶ ἀμφότεροι συντηροῦνται (τηροῦνται D a e): B ℵ L fam. 1 omit.

39. D a b c e ff² omit the verse, and so also apparently Eusebius.

It will be seen that the Sinaitic Syriac (the Curetonian is deficient here, and the Sinaitic after verse 28) habitually goes with B against D; that the larger variants are confined to D and e (the African Old Latin); and that the European Old Latin (occasionally reinforced by ℵ), if they have the divergences at all, have them in a much less pronounced form. It is also significant that some of the larger divergences of D e are due to the substitution (exactly or approximately) of readings found in the parallel passages of the other Synoptics. These divergences are obviously editorial; and this creates some presumption that the other divergences are editorial also. In Acts, where (as may be seen in the examples quoted above, pp. 13–15) the variants are often in the substance of the narrative and not merely verbal, the question is whether the B text or the D text is the original. One or other must be due to editorial action. Since, however, the D text is convicted of editorial

alteration in the Gospels, the presumption is that the same
is the case in Acts.[1]

One thing has long been clear and is generally admitted,
that whatever be the explanation of the non-Neutral early
readings, the term 'Western' is inadequate as a title for
them. Readings of this kind are found, as has been shown,
not only in the Latin authorities, but in Syria and Egypt,
in fact wherever the Gospel text was known. As a result
of the investigation of these readings which has been asked
for, it may be that the term 'Western' may once more
receive a real significance. As has been shown, the readings
of D and the African Old Latin do often hold a place by
themselves, and those of the European Old Latin are allied
to them. It may be that the proposed inquiry would
dissolve the congeries of readings to which the name of
'Western' has been given into a really Western group,
represented mainly by D and the Old Latin version and
Fathers; an Eastern or Syrian group, represented mainly
by the Old Syriac; and an unassorted mass of minor
variants to which no local origin can be assigned, but which
are due to the conditions under which the New Testament
text circulated in the early generations. These are specula-
tions without adequate authority; but it does seem to be
the fact that in a more careful analysis of the non-Neutral
early readings lies the best hope of progress in the establishment of the original text of the New Testament.

All this repeated mention of divergent manuscripts and
families of texts may perhaps give the impression that the
text of the New Testament is abnormally uncertain. Such
an impression can best be corrected by an attempt to
envisage the early history of the text and its present condition. So far from the New Testament text being in an
abnormally unsatisfactory state, it is far better attested

---

[1] Prof. Clark maintains that in Acts (*but not in the Gospels*) the
Western text is original, and the Neutral formed by editorial abbreviation. Ropes, Hort, and most other scholars take the opposite view.

than that of any other work of ancient literature. Its problems and difficulties arise not from a deficiency of evidence but from an excess of it. In the case of no work of Greek or Latin literature do we possess manuscripts so plentiful in number or so near the date of composition. Apart from Virgil, of whom we have manuscripts written some three or four hundred years after the poet's death, the normal position with regard to the great works of classical literature is that our knowledge of their text depends upon a few (or at most a few dozen) manuscripts, of which the earliest may be of the ninth or tenth or eleventh century, but most of the fifteenth. In these conditions it generally happens that scientific criticism has selected one manuscript (usually but not necessarily the oldest) as principal authority, and has based our printed texts on this, with some assistance from the later and inferior manuscripts and a liberal use of conjecture. Recent discoveries of portions of manuscripts of these authors among the papyri of Egypt, which are many centuries older than the vellum manuscripts on which we had previously to base our texts, indicate that reliance on a single early text may be overdone. It is true that the papyri usually confirm the superiority of the manuscript selected by criticism as the best, but the confirmation is not absolute. On the contrary they show that a fair proportion of readings for which the only authority has hitherto been in manuscripts of a late date are in fact early and very probably correct. As a rule it may be said that the support of the papyri is given to the supposedly best manuscript and to the inferior manuscripts respectively in the proportion of about two to one. The papyri have done us the service of enabling us to get behind the previously existing authorities, and to see something of the earlier stages in the formation of the text.

In the case of the New Testament these conditions are reproduced, but on a far higher level of intensity. The vellum manuscripts are far earlier and far more numerous; the gap between the earliest of them and the date of composition of the books is smaller; and a larger number of papyri have (especially since the discovery of the Chester Beatty papyri) given us better means of bridging that gap. We are far better equipped to observe the early stages of textual history in the manuscript period in the case of the New Testament than of any other work of ancient literature.

On the other hand, there are conditions affecting the textual tradition of the New Testament books which differentiate it from all others, and have no doubt tended to complicate it. The works of classical literature have in all probability come down to us mainly through copies made in the great centres of population; and though copies were no doubt (as we see from the papyri) produced locally for local use, it is not likely that they had any influence on the main stream of tradition. With the books of the New Testament the conditions were quite different. During the first three centuries of Christianity, while copies of the Scriptures were required in great numbers, conditions were not favourable to meticulous accuracy of transcription. There was no organized book-trade, distributing authenticated copies of the sacred books from great centres of culture. For the first hundred years, and to a great extent for the first two hundred or two hundred and fifty years, copies of the New Testament books must usually have been produced locally, by local scribes or private individuals. We can imagine a local church or congregation borrowing a copy of a Gospel or an Epistle from its neighbour, and making its own transcript, without much care for precise accuracy. These were not works of literary art; they were the books necessary for salvation, in which the substance was what mattered, not the precise words or the arrangement of them. Scribes at all times and in the most favourable circumstances make mistakes, which can only be corrected by comparison with other copies; and such comparison must often have been difficult, if not impossible, and would not be regarded as very necessary. Further, the best copies would probably be those belonging to the churches and used in the common worship of the congregation; but precisely these would be the object of search in the recurrent periods of persecution, and would be exposed to greater risk of destruction.

In these circumstances we have to envisage the growth, in the second and third centuries, of a large number of local texts, and in the first instance of each Gospel or each small group of Epistles separately. As the papyrus codex came into use (which, as we have seen, may now be ascribed to the third century, and perhaps even to the second), and as at the same time the demand grew for a precise delimitation of the authoritative books of the faith, we must imagine a process of collection of rolls from various sources, of the transcription of the several Gospels into a single codex, and of the commencement of a critical comparison of texts. But not many communities possessed an Origen or even a Clement, and it is reasonable to suppose that the criticism would generally be of a very elementary character. It would be just as likely to take the form of incorporating new incidents or new phrases wherever they were found, or of assimilating the narrative in one Gospel to that in another, as of seeking austerely to preserve an uncontaminated tradition. There was thus every facility for the multiplication of various readings, for the formation of local texts, and very little machinery or desire for their elimination.

To the same period belongs the making of the earliest translations of the sacred books into other languages, Latin, Syriac, and Coptic. Some scholars have imagined an extensive production of bilingual, and even trilingual or quadrilingual, copies of the Scriptures, and a far-reaching contamination of the Greek text thereby. At a later date Graeco-Latin and Graeco-Coptic manuscripts certainly existed, some of which (or fragments of them) have survived; but I find it difficult to believe in any large output of copies demanding so much scholarship and labour. Nor has von Soden's theory of a widespread corruption of

Greek texts by Tatian's Diatessaron found any favour with the scholars best qualified to judge. Nevertheless, while as a rule it would be the Greek text that affected the translation rather than vice versa, some allowance must be made for the perversion of the Greek tradition through this influence.

It would seem, therefore, that there are two stages to be taken into account in explaining the origin of the distinct families of text which we find fully established in the fourth century: the period of casual, unsystematic, and largely unintentional creation of various readings, and the period of conscious, though often very elementary, selection and editorial revision. The creation of variants through scribal errors of course continued at all times, so long as books were copied by hand; but it is only through the earlier part of the second century that it can be supposed to have gone on unchecked. The more the text received definite forms, the less chance had a scribal error or an unauthorized variant of securing admission to the tradition. By the time of Irenaeus and Origen the process of selective criticism had begun; and the manufacture of versions, which must have originated in translations from some definite manuscript or manuscripts, made one particular type of text at least the basis of the Biblical text in that language. It also stands to reason that the comparison of texts and selection among competing readings would be most possible in the greater centres of population, and the results of the process would be more influential there. It is therefore natural to look to such centres as Alexandria in Egypt, Jerusalem and Caesarea in Palestine, Antioch and Edessa in Syria, Carthage in Africa, and Rome in Italy, as likely to be the homes of local editions which would influence the surrounding churches. There is no reason in principle why the same should not be said of such places as Ephesus and other large cities in Asia Minor, Thessalonica in Macedonia, or Corinth in Greece, though no text-families have as yet been associated with them.

The character of such local texts would depend partly on the chance of the material that happened to be available in each centre, and partly on the scholarship of the individual or individuals who undertook the task of selection and revision. There is no reason *a priori* why a text with strongly marked divergences should have existed in northern Africa at the time when the first Latin translation was made, and one rather less strongly marked in Rome, if that was the birthplace of the European Old Latin. All that can be said is that the evidence shows that this was so. There is perhaps a reason why a relatively correct text might be expected in Alexandria, since that was pre-eminently the home of scientific scholarship. But it is quite natural that local texts should come into being independently in places so far apart as Africa, Italy, Egypt, Palestine, and Syria, all ultimately deriving from the early period of uncontrolled production of unrevised manuscripts.

If this is in any degree a truthful picture of the conditions under which the New Testament text was handed down through the second and third centuries, it follows that the presence of readings which can be shown to be of early date in manuscripts containing particularly notable variants is not in itself a proof of the equally early date of these variants. If we find, as we so often do, marked differences in a given passage between the manuscripts B and D, one at least of them must be wrong. This wrong variant must have been introduced by some editor into a text otherwise containing many early and correct readings, but the presence of these early and correct readings is no guarantee of the authenticity of the introduced variant. To take a concrete illustration: the fact that the Chester Beatty papyrus contains many readings which are also found in D is no proof of the authenticity of the larger variants in D and the Old Latin which it does not contain; rather it points to the opposite conclusion, that the text of D and the Old Latin is a secondary development on the basis of an earlier text of which these marked variants did not form part.

It would appear, therefore, that criticism has two distinct kinds of task before it, the one objective in its character and the other subjective. The objective task is to collect and classify readings, to ascertain the earliest date at which they can be shown to have been in existence, and to determine to what local text they belong. This is particularly necessary, as has been indicated above, in the case of the authorities which have been grouped together as 'Western'. Few scholars would now deny that this is not one family but several; and what we need is to know which readings are of local origin, and due to deliberate editorial action, and which are the residue from the earlier period of unassorted readings. So far as appearances at present go, they seem to point to the conclusion that the so-called 'Western' type of text ought to be broken up into at least three local families, African, Italian, and Syriac, with an unassorted residue which is neither eastern nor western, northern or southern, but is found all over the Christian world.

Of the Caesarean text there is not much more to say. Its nucleus has been established, and it is quite possible that further investigation will bring to light other members of the family, or at least other manuscripts in which some Caesarean readings have escaped Byzantine revision. There is also always the hope of more discoveries like that of the Chester Beatty papyrus. First-rate scholars are already at work on the task of reconstructing the Caesarean text from the available materials. There will still remain the task of investigating its origin and character. Is it a text originally formed by editorial scholarship in Palestine, or is it a text brought into Palestine from Egypt? And, so far as it differs from other textual families, are the differences due to editorial revision or to the preservation of authentic original readings?

There remains what is perhaps the most perplexing problem of all, the problem of the Biblical text in Egypt.

It is from Egypt that most of our additional material has come, and from which most is to be expected. The problem has become more complicated since Hort's time. It is no longer a question of a central Egyptian text, represented by B and ℵ, with secondary satellites such as L T Z and their allies. We have the evidence of the Chester Beatty papyrus and perhaps of Origen that the Caesarean text was also in existence there; while the other papyri and the early Egyptian Fathers prove the presence at least of non-Neutral early forms of text, if not of a truly Western type. But the heart of the whole mystery, to which all other inquiries lead up, lies in the answer to the question, What is the character of the B ℵ text? And this question itself has two parts: Is this text intrinsically superior to all others, and, if so, is this superiority due to greater purity of tradition or to a higher measure of editorial scholarship?

In dealing with these questions we reach the subjective side of the textual critic's task. Supposing we have completed, more or less satisfactorily, the isolation of a number of local texts—African, Italian, Syrian, Caesarean, Egyptian, or whatever else they may be—how are we to decide which is the better and the more authentic? Failing the discovery of manuscripts which go close to the date of composition of the New Testament books, the answer must be left to subjective criticism, to our estimate of the intrinsic character of the several types. Which of them, on a comparison of readings, seems most often to present a text which bears the intrinsic signs of authenticity? If any family shows a marked superiority in this respect, we shall be disposed to follow its authority in doubtful cases; though it will be as well to bear in mind the lesson taught by the papyri, as described above (p. 75), that the better manuscript or family is not always right.

On this head we are met by the emphatic opinion of Hort and Weiss, to which reference has already been made, to the effect that the Neutral text, as represented by B, alone bears the signs of having undergone no editorial

M

revision. B has its scribal errors, as every manuscript has; but according to these eminent scholars, it has suffered no material contamination, whether by stylistic revision, or assimilation between parallel texts, or incorporation of extraneous matter. This is a weighty opinion, and it is hard to disprove. Nevertheless, it cannot be said to grow in probability in the light of later knowledge. If the evidence seemed to show that Egypt generally was a country in which the original text was handed down in exceptional purity, it would not be difficult to believe that in B we have a particularly good example of it; but it is now evident that it was not so. Egypt, like other countries, had a variety of texts; and if the text of B is the result of faithful transmission alone, its ancestors must have lived a singularly sheltered life. It is not as if Egypt were the original home of the New Testament books, so that the pure uncorrupted fount was found there. None of them, so far as we know, was written there; most quite certainly were not. The ancestors of the copies current in Egypt must have been a number of separate rolls gathered from many different countries. It is hardly probable that all were of the same type and all arrived uncontaminated; and still less probable that among a number of manuscripts of discordant character one group of rolls of particularly good character, including all the Gospels and Acts and all the Epistles, was kept together, was at some stage copied into a single codex, and so ultimately produced in the fourth century one particularly pure descendant, although at an earlier stage another member of the family (ℵ) had suffered deterioration. It may have been so, but *a priori* probabilities are against it.

If, however, we feel forced to the conclusion that the Neutral text, like the others, is the result of editorial treatment, its character is not thereby ruined, nor does it necessarily fall at once into the same category as the Western or Byzantine texts. There are editors and editors, and editorial handling may take different forms. One editor may set before himself the task of establishing the original text. He will look out for the oldest manuscripts, will try to ascertain which is the best, and will use all the resources of scholarship and textual science to determine in each case which reading has the strongest claim to authenticity. Another may go to work in a quite different spirit, aiming at presenting his text in the most intelligible and attractive form. To him verbal accuracy of tradition is of less importance than practical utility and edification. Particularly might this be the case with the sacred Scriptures. They were not regarded as works of literary art, in dealing with which no one has the right to vary the author's words. Matthew, Luke, and Mark were nothing to the ordinary Christian; they had no copyright, and their feelings as authors did not come into consideration. It was the story of the Master's life and teaching that mattered, and it was desirable that this should be full in matter and easy of comprehension, and that all possibility of offence should be avoided. Hence an editor, or even a copyist who had some power of choice between a number of manuscripts, might with the best intentions in the world take liberties with the text which a literary conscience would condemn. He would smooth down difficult phrases, he would add pronouns or alter the order of words, he would use conventional turns of speech, all in the interests of an easy and comprehensible style. He would be tempted to assimilate the narrative of one Synoptic writer with another, choosing the version which he found fuller or more attractive. He would think he was doing good and not harm if he introduced an occasional incident or piece of local colour which he derived from some other source. Even in the case of the Pauline Epistles, where the personality of the author is more marked, a scribe or editor would be tempted to make verbal alterations in the interest of easier comprehension.

It is in this difference in editorial principle that the difference between the various families is perhaps to be found. The Byzantine text is plainly the result of editorial treatment of the second category. Whether it ever had a clearly marked origin is quite uncertain, but it is certain that the influences that gave rise to it continued to operate, so that its secondary character is intensified. We see it, thanks largely to von Soden's classification, in progressive stages of deterioration, until it attained the form with which we are familiar in the Textus Receptus. Not that it was ever a verbally stereotyped text, but it was a text of an established character, and that a secondary character, in which, while the essential verities were preserved, the verbal expression of them had suffered loss.

In the Western text, in the form to which that term should be confined—the text, that is, which we find in D and other Graeco-Latin manuscripts and in the Old Latin— the hand of the editor is more definitely evident. The divergences between it and the Neutral text are so many and so marked that one or other of them must be due to deliberate editorial action; and considerations of internal probability seem to be decisively in favour of the latter. It is not difficult to understand an editor introducing the passages which are found in D after Matt. xx. 28 or in place of Luke vi. 5; but it would be very hard to understand his omitting them if they were part of the original text. Still more obvious an insertion is that which occurs in W after Mark xvi. 14. Further, as shown above, many of the variations in the Gospels are due to assimilation with the other Synoptics. In Acts they have a different character, resting apparently on personal knowledge of incidents or local circumstances; and if Blass's theory of Luke's own authorship of both versions is not accepted, then the hand of an editor who believed himself to have special knowledge which justified alterations or additions must be recognized.

As opposed to editorial revision of the kind found in the Byzantine and Western families, it seems possible to see in the Caesarean and Neutral texts the hand of an editor who was a scholar, and who was thinking of an authentic text rather than an easy one, of accuracy rather than of edification, or, if the phrase be preferred, of edification through accuracy. The Caesarean text has not yet been fully studied, or indeed fully determined, nor has it been possible as yet to compare its readings in intrinsic quality with those of the Neutral text. So far as appears, however, it does not seem to show either the substantial alterations characteristic of the Western text, or the stylistic and harmonistic alterations of the Byzantine. Whatever may be the final decision as to its originality, it would appear to be a scholarly text, the readings of which deserve respectful consideration. The most marked variation which may belong to the Caesarean text, namely the transference of the *pericope adulterae* from John to some other place in the Gospels (for which there is evidence in Famm. 1 and 13, though not in Θ), would at least be due to a scholar with sufficient sense of style to realize that this paragraph could not be the work of the author of John.

Of the Neutral text, which has been longer known and more completely studied, it can be affirmed with more confidence that, if it is the result of editorial handling, the editor was one who was seeking an original text. It is not harmonistic, it does not cultivate smoothness of phrase, it does not seek additions. It may be described as an austere text. It has indeed been maintained that as between rival texts, the longer one is likely to be the more authentic, since the omission of one or more lines of writing is the besetting sin of scribes. Such a theory, however, can with difficulty be applied to omissions of words which form complete units of sense, unless they can be shown to be cases of homoioteleuton; and it does not seem possible to maintain that the Neutral text could be produced from the fullest Western text by the action of unintentional scribal omissions.

The conclusion, therefore, to which our whole inquiry appears to lead is that for the recovery of the authentic (or the earliest obtainable) text of the New Testament we have to look in the main to the Neutral and Caesarean texts, with such other sporadic readings as can be shown to be of early date. As between these, the choice must be made on considerations of intrinsic character. It is not justifiable, either on the evidence now available with regard to these books, or by analogy with what we now know of the textual history of classical literature in general, to pin our faith on any one manuscript, however high an opinion we may have of its merit. An element of subjective criticism must remain; and this inevitably means an element of uncertainty, since it is impossible to escape the personal equation of the critic. It is better, however, to acknowledge difficulties than to ignore them; and the recognition of the existence of this element of uncertainty may serve to sharpen the wits of critics, and to stimulate the search for objective evidence, which alone can be finally decisive.

Here, for the moment, the story which I have been trying to put together of fifty years of textual criticism comes to an end; but it is not an end which gives the winding up of the story. On the contrary, as I have tried to show, it leaves several large marks of interrogation, to which the attention of scholars is directed. It is very regrettable that the textual criticism of the New Testament does not appear to appeal to the younger generation of scholars so strongly as it did to their predecessors in the nineteenth century. There seem to be lamentably few of the younger scholars who are carrying on the tradition of Lachmann and Tregelles and Tischendorf and Hort and Scrivener and Wordsworth and others of the earlier generation who are still alive. Yet it is a fascinating subject in itself, and one in which much good work remains to be done. It is to be hoped that the discovery of the Chester Beatty papyri, with its mass of new material, may do something to revive interest in a subject of such profound importance as the authentic texts of the original documents of our Christian religion.

Meanwhile, one important task lies ready to hand which

would greatly facilitate the further researches, the necessity of which has been indicated in the previous pages. A new textual apparatus of the New Testament is urgently needed, which, in addition to revising the evidence set out by Tischendorf more than sixty years ago, would incorporate all the new evidence that has been brought to light since that date. The extent and importance of that evidence has been partially indicated in the course of these lectures. Von Soden's edition has not given scholars what they need. It is cumbered by its unfortunate change in the nomenclature of the manuscripts; but still more it is vitiated by the statement of the evidence being subordinated to a classification into groups the validity of which is far from certain. The evidence needs to be stated in the most objective manner possible, leaving students free to make their own deductions from it. At present students have to search for the evidence of the newly discovered witnesses in a score of different volumes, and progressive research is intolerably impeded. Preparations for such a new edition as is required have already been far advanced in this country, and it is to be hoped that publication, even of some part of it, will not be long delayed. The publication even of a single Gospel with an up-to-date apparatus would be of the greatest service, especially if it were the Gospel of St. Mark, in which the textual problems are of special interest; and in due course we might hope to have a complete new critical edition of the New Testament worthy to rank with the Cambridge Septuagint and the Oxford Vulgate, and worthy also of the honourable record of this country in the textual criticism of the Bible.

[It is not possible in the last stages of proof correction to incorporate an examination of the views set out in Prof. A. C. Clark's recent edition of Acts, to which reference has been made in three foot-notes; nor would it show proper respect to a work of so much labour and learning to express a brief judgement on it after a first hasty reading. But it may be observed that it deals primarily with Acts, and that its main conclusion as to the relations between the Western and Neutral texts is expressly said not to apply to the Gospels. How far this weakens the argument with regard to Acts is a point which requires consideration.]

CHAPTER VI

THE GREEK OLD TESTAMENT

THE recent history of the text of the Greek Old Testament has fewer salient features than that of the New. There has been less controversy, but also less progress. There has been less work done, and fewer results or approximations to results. On the other hand, the number of discoveries of new material has been, on the whole, as great, and a description of them and a summary of their results may not be uninteresting.

The point of departure for this survey need not be so far back as in the case of the New Testament. The outstanding event, in which all previous work was summed up and the foundation laid for future progress, was the publication in 1900 of Swete's *Introduction to the Old Testament in Greek*. This was the sequel to the same scholar's manual edition of the text of the Septuagint, which appeared in three volumes in the course of the years 1887–94 (revised edition, 1895–9), and which presented the text of the leading manuscript (B where available, otherwise A or ℵ), with a select apparatus showing the principal variants of the other uncial manuscripts. This edition has provided scholars with a convenient working text, and the *Introduction* summarizes all previous work on the text of the Septuagint. The year 1900 may accordingly be taken as our starting-point.

The several books, or groups of books, of the Old Testament have had different textual histories. Most of the principal manuscripts contain only a portion of the whole Testament, and those which contain the whole are not uniform in character throughout. It is therefore not possible to treat the extant text as one whole. Probably the most convenient method for our present purpose will be, after mentioning certain works of general scope, to describe the principal discoveries of new material during the last thirty-

two years, and then to show, book by book, what results
have been derived from them. Incidentally some idea may
be given of the present state of the textual criticism of the
Greek Old Testament.

The main large-scale work of the last generation, still in
progress, is of course the larger Cambridge edition of the
Septuagint by A. E. Brooke and N. McLean, now respectively Provost of King's and Master of Christ's College,
Cambridge. In this the text is the same (with slight
variations) as in Swete's manual edition, that is, the text
of the Codex Vaticanus, replaced where it is defective by that
of the Alexandrinus or Sinaiticus. The difference is in the
apparatus criticus, which gives the various readings, not merely
of a few uncials, but of all the uncials and a large selection of
minuscules and the available versions and patristic quotations. It is in fact a critical edition on the grand scale,
which replaces the magnificent pioneer work of Holmes and
Parsons (1798–1827). The first part, containing Genesis,
was issued in 1906; the last up to date is the seventh (vol. ii,
part 3), containing 1 and 2 Chronicles, which appeared in
1932. It is a monument of scholarly labour, which does
honour alike to the scholars responsible for it and the
University which publishes it. It does not attempt to pro-
vide a reconstructed text of the Septuagint, but it provides
the materials with which a future generation may achieve
this task.

A beginning has already been made with it. A group of
German scholars at Göttingen, under the leadership of
A. Rahlfs, have planned a critical text of the Septuagint in
sixteen parts, of which the first (Genesis) appeared in
1926. Here the materials gathered together by the Cambridge editors are used, grouped together in families which
aim at representing the texts of Origen, Lucian, and others;
and from them an eclectic text is formed in accordance
with the judgement of the editor. A select critical apparatus is appended. The second part in order of publication,
containing the Psalms, appeared in 1931; and here the

German editors did not have the assistance of the Cambridge collection of materials, which has not yet reached that book. Other parts are announced as being in preparation; so that the next generation may fairly hope to possess a complete *apparatus criticus* for the Septuagint, together with a first attempt at a revised text—a first attempt which, however, cannot hope to be final. The problems of the Septuagint text are too difficult to be solved at once, and more evidence may at any time be forthcoming.

Meanwhile the same group of German scholars have been investigating various details (which cannot be particularized here) in a series of Septuaginta-studien. In this country not much has been done, but it would be wrong not to mention the work of the late Mr. H. St. John Thackeray, whose premature death, shortly after he had joined Messrs. Brooke and McLean in the editorship of the Cambridge Septuagint, was a severe blow to Old Testament scholarship. Not only did he produce an admirable *Grammar of Old Testament Greek* (Cambridge University Press, 1909), in which use was made of the copious evidence with regard to Hellenistic Greek provided by the discoveries of papyri in Egypt, but in the Schweich Lectures for 1920[1] he published the results of his observations (previously notified only in detached articles) of the methods of procedure of the original authors of the Septuagint. It is, of course, universally recognized that the entire Septuagint was not produced at one time—that the Law was first translated, and that the other books followed gradually over a considerable period of years. Analysis of language appears to make quite evident the co-operation of different translators, and that in more ways than one. In the books of Samuel and Kings (as we now call them: the Greek title is Βασιλεῖαι, which Thackeray believes should be rendered 'Reigns', not 'Kingdoms') he finds that the narrative falls into two main portions, one of which is charac-

[1] *The Septuagint and Jewish Worship* (London, British Academy, 1921).

terized by mannerisms of the Palestinian-Asiatic school,
while the other lacks them. He believes that the earlier
translator or (more probably) translators omitted considerable portions of the Hebrew text (viz. 2 Sam. xi. 1–
1 Kings ii. 11, and the last chapter of 1 Kings and the
whole of 2 Kings), which they regarded as unedifying and
as showing the least satisfactory parts of the national
history, and that these were subsequently added by a
different hand or hands. In this later portion he finds much
resemblance to the style of that alternative translation of the
Old Testament which appears to underlie the version of
Theodotion, and of which there are traces in Josephus and
in the New Testament quotations from the Old. From
a curious linguistic usage he even deduces that the home
of this translator was in Western Asia.

In the Prophets he finds a different division of labour.
He believes the earliest stage to have been the rendering
of select passages used as lessons for special festivals; and
that when the complete translation came to be made, the
larger books were habitually divided between two translators. In Jeremiah the division comes in ch. xxix of the
Greek text, in Ezekiel about the beginning of ch. xxviii;
but the second translator in Ezekiel only carried his work
as far as the end of ch. xxxix, after which the first translator
resumed until the end. The division is mechanical, having
no reference to the character of the contents, and probably
represents an original division into two rolls. This seems
probable enough. We have (so far as I know) no evidence
as to the normal length of a Hebrew roll; but half one of
these books corresponds fairly closely with the normal
length of a Greek roll. Thus while the Gospel of St.
Matthew (which may be taken as representing the full
length normally admissible for a Greek roll) contains about
18,000 words (the same as the second book of Thucydides),
the first half of Jeremiah contains about 16,000. Therefore
whether or not the Hebrew rolls were similarly divided, it
is reasonable to suppose that each translator undertook a

portion sufficient to fill one Greek papyrus roll of normal size.[1]

With this tribute to the work of a predecessor in these Lectures, it may be permitted to pass on to a summary enumeration of the principal accretions of textual material which have occurred during the last thirty years, first enumerating the main discoveries, and then considering their bearing on the several books of the Old Testament.

1. *The Freer MSS.*

As mentioned above, in Chapter II, the group of vellum manuscripts acquired in Egypt by Mr. Charles L. Freer in 1906 included two manuscripts of the Old Testament. The first of these, of which a description and collation were published by Prof. H. A. Sanders in 1910,[2] contains the books of Deuteronomy and Joshua. In its present state it consists of 102 leaves of rather thick vellum, measuring about $12\frac{1}{2} \times 10\frac{1}{4}$ inches, with two columns of writing on each page. The 14 quires (originally all of 8 leaves, except the last quire of each book) are numbered from 37 to 50. Thirty-six quires are therefore missing at the beginning, showing that the manuscript originally contained the entire Hexateuch. As each book ends with a small quire and has its last page blank, so as to begin a new book with a new quire, it is possible that Judges and Ruth were originally included, so as to complete the whole Octateuch. This would have resulted in a volume of 57 quires. The script is a large, square, rather heavy uncial, apparently rather later in process of development than the Codex Alexandrinus. It is assigned by Prof. Sanders to the fifth century (and even to the first half of it), by the

---

[1] The evidence for the normal length of Greek papyrus rolls is given in my *Books and Readers in Ancient Greece and Rome* (Oxford, 1932), pp. 51, 52, 62.

[2] *The Old Testament Manuscripts in the Freer Collection*: Part I, *The Washington Manuscript of Deuteronomy and Joshua* (New York, 1910); with complete photographic facsimile published by the University of Michigan.

editors of the New Palaeographical Society to the sixth.
The writing is generally correct. Two double leaves are
missing, containing Deut. v. 16–vi. 18; Joshua iii. 3–iv. 10.
The character of the text will be considered later.

The second Old Testament manuscript in the Freer
collection is a much mutilated copy of the Psalms. When
found, the leaves were adhering together in a solid mass, and
had suffered very greatly from worms, damp, and decay.
The task of separating the leaves was difficult and delicate.
Portions of 107 leaves are preserved, measuring originally
about 14×11 inches; the quires seem to have varied in
size from 6 to 10 leaves. The text is written in single
columns, divided into verses which generally correspond
with the στίχοι of the Codex Vaticanus. The writing is a
large and heavy uncial, nearly square but somewhat
inclined to greater height than width. Prof. Sanders, who
has published a full transcript and description,[1] assigns it
certainly to the fifth century, and is inclined to place it in
the first half. This seems much too early for the character
of the hand, which is more that of the sixth or seventh
century. The manuscript contains Ps. i. 1–cxlii. 8, but all
leaves are imperfect, and of the earlier psalms very little
has survived. The final quire must have been lost early,
and has been replaced by seven leaves from a different
manuscript containing Ps. cxlii. 5–cli. 6, with the first six
verses of the Song of Moses. The addition is in a sloping
hand, apparently of the ninth century.

Ten years after his original purchase of the manuscripts
above described, Mr. Freer acquired in 1916 another manuscript of the Greek Old Testament, this time on papyrus,
containing portions of the Minor Prophets. It consisted
of 28 leaves, all mutilated, with a number of detached
fragments, the work of placing which must have been very
laborious. Ultimately portions of 33 leaves were arranged

[1] *The Old Testament Manuscripts in the Freer Collection*: Part II, *The
Washington Manuscript of the Psalms* (New York, 1917).

in order, containing the text from Hosea xiv. 7 to the end of Malachi, besides a few fragments of the earlier chapters of Hosea. Since the first 18 leaves of the 33 preserved have the *verso* pages preceding the *recto*, while in the remainder *recto* precedes *verso*, it is evident that we have here an example of the early method of forming papyrus codices, in which all the sheets are folded into a single large quire.[1] Allowing 6 leaves for the missing portion of Hosea, the manuscript would have been composed of 24 sheets, folded so as to form 48 leaves or 96 pages. The text of Malachi, however, ends at the bottom of what, on this numeration, would have been p. 78; so that the last 18 pages, or 9 leaves, must either have been blank or contained some other work. As some fragments of papyrus, written in a different hand, and apparently containing a Christian treatise, were found with the Prophets manuscript, they may have belonged to these leaves. The original size of the leaf was about $13\frac{1}{2} \times 6$ inches. The writing is in a single column, with 46–9 lines to the page, in a small script, which may be assigned to the latter part of the third century.

The text has been edited in full by Prof. Sanders, with introduction and specimen facsimiles,[2] and a complete photographic facsimile has been published separately.

In addition to these Greek manuscripts, Mr. Freer's splendid collection at Washington, which has given America an important standing in respect of Biblical manuscripts, contains a Coptic manuscript and some fragments which will be described separately.

2. *The Heidelberg Papyrus*

More than twenty years before the publication of Mr. Freer's manuscript, another papyrus of the Minor Prophets, though much less extensive, had been published at

---

[1] The technique is explained in my *Books and Readers in Ancient Greece and Rome* (Oxford, 1932), pp. 101–7.

[2] *The Minor Prophets in the Freer Collection* (University of Michigan Studies, Humanistic Series, vol. xxi), New York, 1927.

Heidelberg. This consisted of 27 leaves of a papyrus codex, which had been acquired in Egypt in 1889 by the Viennese dealer Theodor Graf, and whose existence was first made known through an article by the chaplain of the British Embassy at Vienna, the Rev. W. H. Hechler, in *The Times* of 1 September 1892. Eventually it was purchased by the Heidelberg University Library, and published in full, with photographic facsimile, by Adolf Deissmann in 1905.[1]

The 27 leaves form portions of 4 quires, two of which were of 8 leaves and two of 10. The column of writing measures approximately $9\frac{1}{2} \times 4\frac{1}{2}$ inches, and the full page probably about 13×7 inches, with 28 lines to the page. The script is a very large and coarse uncial of late date, probably not earlier than the seventh century. The manuscript is consequently a very late survival of the papyrus codex, long after papyrus had been succeeded by vellum as the principal material for book production. Whether the codex originally contained the whole of the Minor Prophets cannot be affirmed in the absence of any page numeration; but it is at least probable. Something like 130 leaves would suffice for the purpose. The leaves actually preserved contain the text from Zech. iv. 6 to Mal. iv. 5, but all are more or less mutilated.

3. *The Berlin Genesis*

The volume of University of Michigan Studies which contained the text of the Freer papyrus of the Minor Prophets included also the text of a papyrus of the book of Genesis, the property of the Berlin Staatsbibliothek. The manuscript was acquired, in extremely bad condition, by Prof. Carl Schmidt in Egypt in 1906, and after various projects for its publication had come to no result, it was eventually jointly edited by Prof. Schmidt and Prof.

---

[1] *Veröffentlichungen aus der Heidelberger Papyrus-sammlung*: I. *Die Septua-ginta-Papyri* (Heidelberg, 1905).

Sanders at the cost of the University of Michigan and the Freer Research and Publication Fund in 1927.

The manuscript, skilfully prepared and mounted by Dr. Ibscher, consists now of 16 leaves of papyrus, 9 of which are written in double columns and the rest in single columns. Originally there must have been 32 leaves, arranged in a single quire. The scribe evidently had to accommodate his text to his papyrus, hence his change to single columns and a greater crowding of the writing in the latter part of the manuscript. The column of writing measures about $8\frac{1}{2} \times 6\frac{3}{4}$ inches; the size of the margins cannot be determined, but the total size of the page may have been about $11 \times 8\frac{1}{2}$ inches. The number of lines varies between 28 and 37, from 30 to 32 being the most usual; but there is great irregularity in the number of letters contained in a line. In short, the manuscript is far from being a good example of formal book-production.

The hand is cursive, documentary rather than book-hand, and consequently easier to date with some approach to confidence. It shows much resemblance to papyrus documents written in the early part of the fourth century, though Prof. Sanders would place it at the end of the third.

The text includes Gen. i. 16 (the first leaf being lost)– xxv. 8, and at the end has the title γένεσις κόσμου, which seems to indicate that this was the end of the codex, as it certainly was of the quire. The rest of the book was no doubt contained in another single-quire codex, which (since only one-third of the book remains to be provided for) may have made a beginning with Exodus also. The break comes in the middle of a verse, so is evidently quite arbitrary. The manuscript would therefore appear to be another example of the practice, noted by Mr. Thackeray, of dividing the longer books into two portions. There would have been no difficulty in getting the whole book into a single volume of about 50 leaves, for single-quire codices of much greater extent are now known (notably among the Chester Beatty papyri); but Gen. i. 1–xxxv. 8

is about the normal length of a papyrus roll, and this codex was no doubt copied from such a roll.

4. *The Chester Beatty Papyri*

To this already imposing quantity of new material has now come the magnificent addition of the Chester Beatty papyri, a list of which has already been given (above, pp. 52–3). As there set out, they comprise portions of eight distinct codices, and include some part of the text of nine different books, Genesis, Numbers, Deuteronomy, Isaiah, Jeremiah, Ezekiel, Daniel, Esther, and Ecclesiasticus. There are two manuscripts of Genesis, one containing about two-thirds of the book on 44 double-columned leaves, the other about a quarter of it on 22 single-columned leaves in a cursive hand. The former is in a formal uncial of the fourth century, the latter in a document hand probably of the end of the third. The Numbers-Deuteronomy papyrus is a beautifully written manuscript, double-columned, in a fine, small book-hand which seems certainly to be of the second century, and therefore is the earliest extant manuscript of any part of the Greek Bible. It is, unfortunately, torn into a multitude of fragments, but substantial portions of 33 leaves have been preserved, and 22 more can be identified. The Isaiah is sadly mutilated; 27 leaves are represented, but of none is more than half preserved, and of many much less. It is elegantly written, and has a few marginal notes, some of them Coptic; the date appears to be third century. Of Jeremiah there is only part of one leaf, of about the same date. Ezekiel and Esther, though written in different hands, probably of the second half of the third century, form a single codex, of which 16 leaves have survived out of an original total of about 78, of which the last four must have been blank or contained some other text. Of Daniel 13 leaves are preserved, but nearly half of each is lost; the page numeration shows that some other book must have preceded. The writing is an extremely clear hand, probably of the first half of the third century.

Finally, of Ecclesiasticus there is only one complete leaf and part of a second, in a rough hand of the fourth century.

Collectively the Chester Beatty papyri form a wonderful addition to our textual material for the Septuagint, besides throwing much light on the methods of book-production in the early centuries of the Christian era. Their textual character will be considered below, under the respective books to which they belong.

5. *Minor Papyrus Manuscripts and Fragments*

Among the papyrus and vellum fragments discovered in the course of excavations in Egypt, quite a considerable number contain portions of the Old Testament. They are, in fact, rather more numerous than the similar fragments of the New. Mr. Hedley's unpublished catalogue, referred to above (p. 32, note 1), enumerates 174 fragments of the Old Testament, as against 157 of the New. It cannot be said that they are of much importance, and a brief mention of a few of them will be sufficient here. The book most frequently represented is, perhaps not unnaturally, the Psalms. Of this there are two papyri of some length. One, at Leipzig, is a roll about 13 feet 6 inches long, which on the *recto* contains a document dated A.D. 338, and on the *verso* (and consequently of later date, presumably the second half of the fourth century) Ps. xxx–lv, the first five psalms being considerably mutilated.[1] Another Psalter of some extent is papyrus 37 in the British Museum, acquired so long ago as 1836 from the ruins of an Egyptian monastery; it consists of 32 leaves containing Ps. xi. 2–xxxiv. 6, written in an irregular hand of rather Coptic character, apparently of the seventh century.[2] Papyrus 980 of the Società Italiana is two leaves of a papyrus codex of the late third or fourth century, containing Ps. cxliii. 14–cxlviii. 3, with

[1] Edited by C. F. Heinrici, *Beiträge zur Geschichte und Erklärung des A.T.*, pt. iv (1903).

[2] Edited by Tischendorf, *Monumenta Sacra Inedita*, nov. coll. i. 217; description and specimen plate in *Catalogue of Ancient MSS. (Greek) in the British Museum.*

a text of some interest. The rest are all small fragments
of little importance.

Of the other books, Genesis is the one that occurs most
frequently. Oxyrhynchus pap. 656, consisting of parts of
four leaves of a papyrus codex, contains Gen. xiv. 21–3,
xv. 5–9, xix. 32–xx. 11, xxiv. 28–47, xxvii. 32, 33, 40, 41,
and is assigned by the editors to the first half of the third
century. It is written in a square, well-formed hand,
which might be even earlier. Its age gives it importance,
though it is now somewhat overshadowed by the Berlin
and Chester Beatty papyri of this book. It is, however, even
earlier than these, and is perhaps the earliest extant manuscript of the Greek Bible, with the exception of the Chester
Beatty Numbers-Deuteronomy. The other Genesis fragments are too small to be of much textual value, but two
of them have features of special interest. One, a tiny scrap
in the Amherst collection, contains the first five verses of
Genesis in both the Septuagint version and that of Aquila,
written on the back of a roll in a hand apparently of the
early fourth century. It adds a few words to the extant
text of Aquila, and is at any rate a curiosity. The other
(Oxyrhynchus pap. 1073) is a leaf of a vellum codex,
probably of the fourth century, with a few verses of Genesis
(v. 4–13, 29–vi. 2) in the Old Latin version, with some
otherwise unknown readings.

None of the other papyrus fragments of the Old Testament is sufficiently large or important for separate notice.
Some of them are too small to have any discernible character at all. Of the rest it can only be said, as has been said
already in regard to the New Testament, that they show
that there was no one standard form of text current in
Egypt. Several of them agree generally with the Vaticanus,
but others show agreements rather with the Sinaiticus or
Alexandrinus. Collectively they show that in the third
and fourth centuries various textual traditions were on
foot, and that it is a mistake to pin one's faith to any single
authority.

6. *The Coptic Versions*

The Coptic contributions to the textual history of the Old Testament are considerable in extent and important in quality. Since the Coptic versions were unquestionably translated from the Greek, they are valuable evidence for the text of the Septuagint as current in Egypt in the early Christian centuries. The earliest in date is a manuscript in the British Museum (Or. 7594), to which reference has already been made, a papyrus codex containing a curious combination of books, Deuteronomy, Jonah, and Acts, which is approximately datable to the first half of the fourth century. This was acquired by the Museum in 1911, and edited by Sir E. Budge.[1] Next in importance is a complete Psalter (Or. 5000), published by the same editor in 1898,[2] probably of about the seventh century. Another very substantial volume (Or. 5984), of about the same date, originally contained all the Sapiential books; 62 leaves now survive, containing considerable portions of Proverbs, Ecclesiastes, Song of Solomon, Wisdom, and Ecclesiasticus, with a small fragment of Job.[3] All of these are in the Sahidic dialect, the Bohairic MSS. in the Museum having all been acquired at dates before 1900.

The Freer collection also includes one important Coptic manuscript, besides a number of fragments. This is a vellum Psalter, acquired in 1908, composed of extremely small leaves, measuring about $3\frac{1}{8} \times 2\frac{3}{4}$ inches. A complete Psalter would have required about 380 such leaves, but it may have been divided into two or more volumes. The Freer MS., which may perhaps be assigned to the sixth century, contains portions of pages 17 to 258, with the text (much mutilated at the beginning and end) of Ps. vi. 5–liii. 3. It was fully published by W. H. Worrell

---

[1] *Coptic Biblical Texts in the Dialect of Upper Egypt* (London, 1912).

[2] *The Earliest Known Coptic Psalter* (London, 1898).

[3] Described, with all the other Coptic manuscripts in the Museum, by W. E. Crum, in his *Catalogue of the Coptic Manuscripts in the British Museum* (London, 1905); edited by Sir H. Thompson (Oxford, 1908).

in 1916, and again, with the other Coptic manuscripts in the collection, in 1923.[1] The other manuscripts include fragments of Job and of another Psalter, also on very small vellum pages.

The Chester Beatty collection includes, in addition to the Greek manuscripts already described and the Coptic manuscripts of the New Testament, a volume containing the first fifty Psalms; and the remainder of this Psalter is at Michigan. These have not yet been edited.

At Berlin there is a fragmentary Coptic Psalter, which Rahlfs assigns to about A.D. 400,[2] and which he has edited and used in his edition of the Psalms for the Göttingen Septuagint.

The great Pierpont Morgan collection of papyri, discovered in 1910, includes three Old Testament manuscripts on vellum, in the Sahidic dialect. One, of the eighth or ninth century, contains Leviticus, Numbers, and Deuteronomy; one, dated A.D. 893, 1 and 2 Samuel; and one, of the eighth or ninth century, Isaiah. A check-list of the collection has been published (1919), and a complete set of photographic facsimiles, but I know of no study of the character of the texts. They must therefore for the present be left out of account.

From the foregoing brief summary of the recent accretions of textual material, it is clear that substantial additions have been made since 1900 to the means at the disposal of scholars for dealing with the problems of Septuagint criticism. The text of the Septuagint cannot, however, be dealt with as a single proposition. The several books comprising the Old Testament were translated at different times and by different hands; and there is even less assurance than in the New Testament that the

---

[1] *The Coptic Psalter in the Freer Collection* (University of Michigan Studies, Humanistic Series, vol. x, pt. 1 (1916)); *The Coptic Manuscripts in the Freer Collection* (New York, 1923).

[2] *Die Berliner Handschrift des sahidischen Psalters* (Abhandlungen der Ges. d. Wiss. zu Göttingen, 1901).

character of any given manuscript is uniform throughout the whole of its contents. Each book or group of books has its own textual problems; and with the exception of the few great 'pandects' containing the entire Testament, the textual authorities available for the several books differ materially. In considering, therefore, the textual results to be derived from the new material, it is necessary to take the books separately, and to see how each is affected by the new evidence. Only those books will be discussed in which the new material is substantial enough to be of real importance.

For the benefit of those who are not familiar with the subject, it may be as well to prefix a brief indication of the principal problems, arising out of the history of the translation, with which the textual critic has to deal. Ancient tradition, embodied primarily in the document known as the Letter of Aristeas, which purports to be written by a Greek official in the court of Ptolemy Philadelphus (285–247 B.C.), assigns its origin to the reign of that king and to his instigation; and though the Letter cannot be depended on for accuracy in detail, there is no reason to doubt that at least the Books of the Law were translated at that time and in Alexandria. The other books followed in the course of the next century and a half, the last being Ecclesiasticus, the prologue to which (written probably in 132 B.C.) speaks of 'the Law itself and the Prophets and the rest of the books' as being already translated. The translation thus produced comprised all the books which were then regarded as coming within the canon of the sacred scriptures, which was considerably more extensive than what we now know as the Old Testament. About the last years of the first century of the Christian era, a generation after the destruction of Jerusalem, a school of Hebrew scholars at Jamnia appear to have revised the canon, excluding from it those books and portions of books which now appear in our Bible as the Apocrypha.[1] This exclusion, however, was not

[1] Throughout the Middle Ages these books, being included in the

recognized by the Christian Church as a whole, and from this point onward there is a difference in content between the Greek Old Testament and the Hebrew; and the more the Christian Church was attached to the Septuagint, the less willing were the Jews to admit its authority.

The non-Palestinian Jews, however, who had little knowledge of Hebrew, had need of a Greek translation of their Scriptures, while many of the Christians also respected the decisions of the Hebrew scholars. Accordingly in the course of the second century three new translations were produced, which followed the Hebrew canon. These were the work of Aquila, Theodotion, and Symmachus. That of Aquila was characterized by slavish fidelity to the Hebrew, to the extent of the violation of Greek grammar and syntax in order to follow the idiosyncrasies of the Hebrew. The version of Theodotion was apparently due to a recognition by a part at least of the Christian community of the authority of the Hebrew canon. Its author was an Ebionite Christian, and his version follows the Hebrew canon, but is written in better Greek than that of Aquila and agrees more closely with the Septuagint. There is, moreover, some evidence that it was based on an earlier translation, since quotations in the New Testament and in some of the early Fathers often agree with it. It found favour in the Christian Church, and in the book of Daniel it superseded the Septuagint version; and there is some reason to believe that the same was the case with Ezra and Nehemiah and perhaps Chronicles (the version which stands in our Apocrypha as 1 Esdras being the original Septuagint). The version of Symmachus, which is probably the latest of the three, again follows the Hebrew canon, but aims at a more idiomatic Greek, and it never acquired the authority of

Vulgate (though Jerome himself preferred the Hebrew canon), were an integral part of the Bible of the Christian Church; but the English translators followed Luther in relegating to a separate category (the Apocrypha) the books and portions of books not included in the Hebrew canon.

Aquila among the Jews or of Theodotion among the Christians.

None of these three versions now exists in its entirety, or as a continuous text at all except in the books just mentioned which were adopted from Theodotion. Our knowledge of them is chiefly due to the work of the great scholar Origen (A.D. 185–253), who produced a six-fold edition of the Old Testament known as the Hexapla, in which he set out in six parallel columns (1) the Hebrew text, (2) the same transliterated in Greek characters, (3) the version of Aquila, (4) Symmachus, (5) a text composed by himself, (6) Theodotion. Origen's own text was the Septuagint, corrected to some extent to correspond with the Hebrew, in which passages present in the LXX but wanting in the Hebrew were marked by an obelus (— or ÷), while passages present in the Hebrew but wanting in the LXX were supplied from Aquila or Theodotion and marked by an asterisk. It was a deliberate attempt by a great scholar to produce a revised Septuagint more in accordance with the Hebrew text as then fixed by Jewish scholars.

No copy of the complete Hexapla now exists, but a separate edition of Origen's text was produced by Pamphilus and Eusebius at Caesarea early in the fourth century; and at the same time two other editions of the Septuagint were produced, which have left their mark on the textual tradition. One was by Hesychius at Alexandria, the other by Lucian at Antioch. The problem of the textual critic to-day is therefore to try to disentangle from the extant manuscripts and versions the several editions of Origen, Lucian, and Hesychius, and so far as may be to arrive at the pre-Origenian text of the Septuagint. If that could be done, there would still remain the problem of the relation of the Septuagint to the original Hebrew, and the question whether the Septuagint does or does not prove the existence, in the third and second centuries before Christ, of a Hebrew text differing materially from that fixed by the Jewish scholars at Jamnia, and thenceforth transmitted in what is known as the Massoretic text, which appears in all extant Hebrew manuscripts and is translated in our English Bibles. This, however, is outside our present subject.

With this preface[1] it may be easier to understand the bearing of the new evidence which will now be considered in connexion with the several books affected by the discoveries described in the preceding pages.

Genesis

The book of Genesis has been particularly fortunate in the extent of the new discoveries of manuscripts; and this is the more welcome because it previously stood at a disadvantage. Neither of the two earliest of the great vellum manuscripts was available for it to more than a very small extent. In the Codex Vaticanus the greater part of the book is wanting, up to xlvi. 28, while in the Sinaiticus nothing has survived except a fragment containing xxiii. 19–xxiv. 46. The earliest substantial authority was therefore the Alexandrinus, which is complete with the exception of a few verses in chs. xiv–xvi. The other principal authorities were the Cotton Genesis (D) of the fifth century, the evidence of which rests upon a careful collation made before its almost complete destruction in the fire at Ashburnham House in 1731; the Bodleian Genesis (E), of the ninth or tenth century, which is defective in chs. xiv–xviii, xx–xxiv, and from xlii. 18 to the end; the Ambrosianus (F), of the fifth century, which begins at xxxi. 15; the Sarravianus (G), of the fifth century, for the small portion xxxi. 54–xxxvi. 18; the scattered fragments of the Vienna Genesis (L), of the fifth to sixth century; and the Codex Coislinianus (M), of the seventh century. To these have now to be added the two Chester Beatty papyri and the

---

[1] For a fuller statement of the facts here summarized, Swete's *Introduction* should be consulted, where descriptions of the several manuscripts will be found. For a more popular but second-hand account, reference may be made to my *Bible and the Ancient Manuscripts* (3rd ed., 1898).

Berlin papyrus, which are from a hundred to a hundred and fifty years older than the earliest of these, and the Oxyrhynchus fragment, which may be as much as two hundred years older.

The first point that emerges from an examination of the new witnesses is that a considerable affinity exists between the three larger ones (the two Chester Beatty papyri, designated 961 and 962, and the Berlin papyrus, designated 911). The agreement between 961 and 962, even in unique or almost unique readings, is so strong that they must have had a common ancestor at no very remote interval. With 911 their agreement, if not quite so pronounced, is at any rate much stronger than with any other manuscript, except (significantly enough) the minuscule manuscript known as 135, which is regarded as a leading representative of the text of Origen. They also show a high proportion of agreements with G, which is also Origenian, in the small number of readings where it is extant. As compared with the vellum uncials, they show a much higher proportion of agreements with D and M than with A, and only a somewhat smaller measure of agreement with E.

The Oxyrhynchus fragment (U_4 in Brooke and McLean's edition), on the other hand, does not fall into this group. In the few passages where both are extant, U_4 differs from 961 more often than it agrees with it. Only once does it agree with 961 (and 135) against the other authorities, and twice when the support of other uncials is small. It is evident that on the whole it represents a different family of text.

So far therefore as Genesis is concerned, it would appear that our main gain is a strong reinforcement of the authorities for the type of text identified with Origen; a conclusion not unlike that at which we arrived in connexion with the Chester Beatty Gospels manuscript.

Numbers

The Chester Beatty papyrus of the fourth and fifth books of the Pentateuch originally contained (as is shown by the page numeration) the complete text of Numbers and Deuteronomy. The extant portion of Numbers consists mainly of v. 12–viii. 19, with smaller fragments of other chapters, especially xxv. 18 to the end. The textual questions with regard to this book are not important, but a comparison of the evidence of the papyrus in the two books is instructive with regard to the textual history of the Septuagint in general. The principal manuscripts for comparison are A B F G as before; a palimpsest at Leningrad (H), of the sixth century, which contains considerable portions of the book; and the minuscules 54, 75, and a_2, the latter being the minuscule continuation of the uncial manuscript which in Genesis is known as E. An analysis of the various readings in these manuscripts shows that the papyrus is most often in agreement with B and a_2. The Hexapla manuscript G comes next, and then F; then 54, 75, H, and A, in that order. The papyrus has few readings peculiar to itself. This grouping of manuscripts has no particular interest in itself; but it becomes of significance when compared with the grouping revealed in Deuteronomy.

Deuteronomy

Deuteronomy is one of the books which has profited most by the discovery of new manuscripts; for besides the Chester Beatty papyrus (963), which is of the second century, there is the Freer vellum manuscript of the fifth or sixth century (Θ), and the British Museum Coptic papyrus of the fourth. The principal manuscripts previously known are those just enumerated for Numbers, except that H drops out. Now when the readings of the Chester Beatty MS. are compared with these, its affinities are found to be totally different from those shown in Numbers. B, instead of being at the head of the list in agreements, is at the bottom, and a_2 is no longer so closely associated with it. A and F are considerably nearer to the papyrus; but its closest relations are with G (which is only extant for a small part of the book), Θ, 54, 75, and a₂. The connexion between Θ, 54, and 75 had already been noticed by Prof. Sanders in his edition of the Freer MS. It may be observed that in Genesis Rahlfs regards 75 as a typically Lucianic manuscript, while 54 is said to be Origenian in the first half of the book and to have a different character in the second half. In Deuteronomy, however, they are generally found in the same group, by whatever name it is to be labelled; and Θ and the Chester Beatty MS. often join them. It has been noted that 963 also shows much agreement with G; but this is by no means always in the readings which it shares with 54 and 75. It would not appear, therefore, that Θ-54-75-963 are to be regarded as forming an Origenian group along with G. The conclusion would rather be that 963 at any rate represents one of the families of text which Origen had before him in preparing his own edition. It cannot be Lucianic or Hesychian, since it is before the date of these editions.

The state of things here disclosed emphasizes the warning already given that the character of a manuscript cannot be counted on to be constant throughout. The affinities of 963 in Numbers and Deuteronomy respectively are quite different. It was no doubt copied from two (or more) distinct rolls; and these chanced to be of different textual character. 54 and 75, also, which appear to be of different families in Genesis, are allies in Deuteronomy. Θ-54-75 may apparently be regarded as an allied group, but 963, which is considerably earlier, goes back before the formation of the principal families, and represents one of the texts out of which they were made.

Another point which is of some interest is that, since 963 gives support to the A text in Deuteronomy and the B text in Numbers, it appears to show that both these types of text existed already in the second century, so that neither can claim preference on the ground of superior antiquity.

The British Museum Coptic MS. was not available for

use by Brooke and McLean in this book, but a collation of it is attached to the prefatory note of their part iv (Joshua, &c.). Like 963 and Θ, it agrees decidedly with A F rather than with B, a consensus of early evidence which goes far to support the A text rather than B in this book. In the order of the Commandments, however, it agrees with B against A F in placing the seventh before the sixth.

Joshua

The historical books of the Old Testament seem to have been little read or copied among the Greek-speaking population of Egypt; for among all the fragments found at Oxyrhynchus, and those in the British Museum, Amherst, Rylands, and Florence collections, they are represented only by one small vellum scrap of Joshua and one of Judges, with nothing from the books of Samuel, Kings, and Chronicles. Joshua is, however, represented by the Freer MS. (Θ) which also contains Deuteronomy. This contains the whole of the book with the exception of the two leaves on which was written iii. 2–iv. 10. Its textual relations are not the same as in Deuteronomy. It still agrees with A much oftener than with B, and this agreement is specially marked in the forms of proper names; but it parts company with 54 and 75. F (which is only extant for part of the book) is less closely associated with A, and has more agreements with B. On the whole, the characters of the various manuscripts in this book, and their relations to the several editions of Origen, Hesychius, and Lucian, are rather obscure, and need further investigation.

Psalms

The Psalter, owing to its popularity both for liturgical and for private use, is by far the most fully provided with textual evidence of all the books of the Old Testament; but as in the similar case of the Gospels, by far the greater number of manuscripts represent a relatively late recension, generally adopted for use in the Church. Rahlfs reckons the following main textual families: (1) the Lower Egyptian text, represented by B א and the Bohairic version; (2) the Upper Egyptian text, represented by the Sahidic version, the British Museum papyrus 37 (U), and the Leipzig papyrus edited by Heinrici (2013); (3) the Western text, represented by the Verona Graeco-Latin Psalter of the sixth century (R) and a Latin Psalter at St. Germain-des-Prés of the same date; (4) the Origenian text, represented by Hexapla fragments at Milan and Cambridge and Jerome's Gallican Psalter; (5) the Lucianic recension, found in the vast majority of manuscripts; and (6) an early unclassified text, represented by A, the Freer Psalter, and a tenth-century minuscule at Rome (55).

That the common ecclesiastical text is rightly identified with the edition of Lucian seems to be established by its agreement with the texts used by Theodoret and Chrysostom, both of whom are associated (like Lucian) with Antioch, and with the text used by Jerome's correspondents Sunnia and Fretela, which Jerome expressly calls Lucianic. The Lower Egyptian text appears to be pre-Origenian and unrevised. The Upper Egyptian text is marked by a considerable number of additions of definitely Christian character (e.g. the addition to Ps. xiii. 1–3, which St. Paul quotes in Rom. iii. 10, 11, of a number of passages elsewhere in the Psalms which St. Paul appends without break of continuity); many of these, but not all, found their way into the other texts. Whether the edition of Hesychius can be identified with any of these types of text seems uncertain, but Rahlfs is of opinion that Hesychius took over the pre-Origenian text with little alteration.

From the above enumeration it will be seen that the recently discovered manuscripts described in the first part of this chapter have aided materially in establishing the principal families of the Psalter text. The Upper Egyptian text, in particular, rests mainly on the British Museum Coptic Psalter, the Berlin Coptic MS., the Freer Coptic MS., and the Leipzig papyrus of Heinrici, with the addition of the previously known British Museum papyrus 37. The Freer Greek Psalter joins with A as a witness to a separate type of early date, the origin of which is uncertain. None of them, however, join the Lower Egyptian group, which has the highest claim to originality; though this, too, includes a number of Christian additions. The Coptic Psalter which is divided between Mr. Chester Beatty and the University of Michigan has not yet been published, but may be presumed to belong to the Sahidic group.

Esther

The Chester Beatty papyrus 967, in which the books of Ezekiel and Esther were combined, has eight leaves containing Esther ii. 20–viii. 6, but the lower half of each leaf is lost. The only uncials for comparison are ℵ A B, and the affinities of the papyrus are not doubtful. It has about forty readings peculiar to itself, but in readings which it shares with the uncials it agrees emphatically with ℵ B against A. The variations and additions which are characteristic of the corrector of ℵ known as ℵ$^{c, a}$ do not appear in it.

The Major Prophets

For all the Major Prophets we have some accession of material from the Chester Beatty papyri, but nothing of any importance from any other source. The Isaiah (965) is unfortunately only a collection of fragments, in no case exceeding half of a leaf and generally much less. The four uncials for comparison are ℵ A B Q, and of these ℵ A Q, though not constantly agreeing among themselves, tend to combine against B. The papyrus falls into the same group, agreeing about equally with the three uncials, and disagreeing oftener than not with B. It agrees slightly more with the Marchalianus (Q), which is believed to represent the text of Hesychius, than with ℵ A, but the difference is very small. Its own peculiar readings are not of much importance; but in a few cases it agrees with the

Giotta Ferrata palimpsest (Γ) against all the other four uncials.

The Jeremiah fragment is too small to establish the character of the papyrus. All that can be said is that it twice agrees with א A Q against B.

Of Ezekiel, as of Esther, eight continuous leaves are preserved, but rather less than half of each leaf is lost. Here A B Q are again available for comparison, and Γ for a small part of the text; but א is not represented. The relations of this papyrus (967) with them are totally different from those of 965 in Isaiah. Here the predominance of agreement is emphatically with B, and to an almost equal extent with Γ where that is extant. There is a preponderance of agreement over disagreement with Q, though not to anything like the same extent, while A is by far the least in favour. Peculiar readings are fairly plentiful in number, and prove the independent character of the papyrus; but they are not important in character.

For Daniel the Chester Beatty papyrus (968) is of quite exceptional importance. As mentioned above, the original Septuagint version of this book did not win favour in the Christian Church, and was superseded by that of Theodotion, which is found in every extant manuscript of the Greek Bible containing this book, with a single exception. The original Septuagint has therefore been known to us hitherto solely from this one copy, a minuscule manuscript in the Chigi Library at Rome, variously assigned to the ninth or eleventh century, with assistance from a Syriac translation of a Hexaplaric text at Milan. It was therefore highly interesting to find that the new papyrus did not contain the Theodotionic text but the LXX. About five chapters are preserved, with the loss, however, of nearly half of each leaf. The most notable variation is in the order of the chapters, chs. vii and viii being placed before v. The several episodes are numbered, the number 3 being prefixed to ch. iv, 5 to ch. viii, and 7 to ch. v. The other

numbers are lost.[1] In the main, it confirms the accuracy
of the Chigi MS., for though there are about 180 variations
in text, they are mostly small in extent and of no great
importance. In several places words which are marked
with an asterisk in the Chigi MS. or the Syriac (and which
therefore formed no part of the original LXX) are
omitted.

Minor Prophets

For the Minor Prophets we have the Freer MS. of the
third century, which contains (subject to mutilations) all
the books except the greater part of Hosea, the Heidelberg
papyrus of Zechariah and Malachi of the seventh, and the
British Museum Coptic papyrus of Jonah of the fourth.
The Freer MS. (W), which is the most important, shows
about thirty instances of agreement with the Hebrew as
against the other Greek authorities, with a few readings
which may have been derived from Symmachus or Aquila.
As its editor, Prof. Sanders, remarks, this is sufficient to
show that accommodation of the Greek text to the Hebrew
was not confined to Origen, and did not begin with him,
but was an influence to which Greek manuscripts of the
LXX were at all times liable. Its occurrence is therefore
not necessarily a proof of Hexaplaric influence. The
uncials available for comparison are A B Q in Amos and
Micah, ℵ A B Q in the other books. Of these Q is the
one with which the Freer MS. shows the greatest measure
of agreement, with B next, and ℵ decidedly the least.
But the important fact emerges that the Freer MS. is to
a considerable extent independent of all of these. It has
no less than 500 readings which are not found in any of
the uncials, and for about half of these support is found
among the minuscules. Five minuscule manuscripts show
more agreements with W than do Q and B, those namely
which are known as 407, 198, 233, 534, and 410; and these

---

[1] Ch. vii would no doubt have been section 4, but it is not clear
what section 6 was, as ch. v follows directly on viii.

are manuscripts which are regarded as representing pre-dominantly the pre-Hexaplaric text. 407 and 410 are closely related, especially in the books Joel-Malachi (which in the LXX follow Hosea, Amos, and Micah), and the combination of so early a witness as W with them adds great weight to the group. If Sanders is right in finding a closer affinity in this group with the Achmimic or Middle Egyptian version than with either Sahidic or Bohairic, the home of the group may be looked for in Middle Egypt.

The Heidelberg papyrus is stated by Deissmann to belong to the Hesychian group, headed by A and Q, with the minuscules 106, 49, and 26. With these it shows a much higher proportion of agreements than with any other manuscript; and it agrees much less with B than does W. In fact a combination of the Heidelberg MS. with A Q against B W is a rather common phenomenon. The late date of the papyrus, however, makes its evidence of less importance.

The Jonah Coptic papyrus is said also to show many small variants in common with A and Q, but I do not know that it has been carefully examined by any Septuagint scholar.

Sapiential Books

The Sapiential or Solomonic books are represented mainly by the British Museum Coptic MS. (p. 100), containing portions of Proverbs, Ecclesiastes, Song of Solomon, Wisdom, and Ecclesiasticus. Sir H. Thompson says of its text merely that in Wisdom it is not so good as the Turin MS., but in Ecclesiasticus it often comes nearer to the Greek uncials. The small Chester Beatty fragment of two leaves of Ecclesiasticus is not extensive enough to allow of any very definite conclusions. So far as it goes, it appears to adhere regularly to none of the principal authorities, but to go rather oftener with B than with ℵ, A, or C.

The foregoing conspectus of the additions to textual knowledge of the Septuagint since 1900 is rather a statement of problems than a solution of them. It rests on the conclusions (often partial and provisional) of the first editors of the various manuscripts which have come to light, and on a first examination of the most recent discoveries of all, the Chester Beatty papyri. It will have been more useful if it encourages some younger scholars to join the small band of those who, at home or abroad, are dealing with the complicated problems of the text of the Greek Old Testament. It was to encourage research, as well as to make the results of research generally known, that the enlightened benefactors of the British Academy founded the Schweich Lectures.

INDEX

PRINTED IN
GREAT BRITAIN
AT THE
UNIVERSITY PRESS
OXFORD
BY
JOHN JOHNSON
PRINTER
TO THE
UNIVERSITY